THE ROARING TWENTIES

DISCOVER THE ERA OF PROHIBITION, FLAPPERS, AND JAZZ

Marcia Amidon Lusted
Illustrated by Jennifer K. Keller

Nomad Press
A division of Nomad Communications
10 9 8 7 6 5 4 3 2 1

This book was manufactured by TC Transcontinental Printing,
Beauceville Québec, Canada
August 2014, Job #67280
ISBN: 978-1-61930-264-8

Illustrations by Jennifer K. Keller
Educational Consultant, Marla Conn

Questions regarding the ordering of this book should be addressed to
Nomad Press
2456 Christian St.
White River Junction, VT 05001
www.nomadpress.net

Printed in Canada.

~ Titles in the *Inquire and Investigate* Series ~

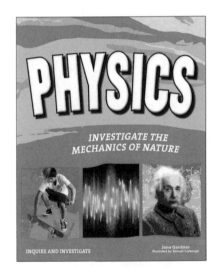

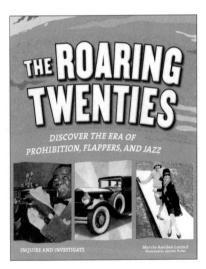

Contents

1918, November 11..... World War I ends on the 11th hour of the 11th day of the 11th month.

1919, January 16........ Congress ratifies the 18th Amendment, prohibiting the sale of alcohol in the United States.

1920 .... For the first time, the United States census reports that more Americans live in urban areas than rural areas.

1920, March 19 .... The U.S. Senate refuses to participate in the League of Nations.

1920, August 18......... Congress ratifies the 19th Amendment, giving women the right to vote.

1921, May 19 .... Congress passes limitations on European immigration to the United States.

1921, May 31 .... The trial of Sacco and Vanzetti begins.

1921, September 7–8 .. The first Miss America Pageant is held in Atlantic City, New Jersey.

1922, February 5 .... The first issue of *Reader's Digest* is published.

1922, May 30 .... The Lincoln Memorial in Washington, DC, is dedicated.

1923 .... Yankee Stadium is built in the Bronx, New York.

1923, March 2 .... *Time* Magazine is published for the first time.

1923, August 2 .... Calvin Coolidge becomes president after the death of President Warren G. Harding.

1923 .... Clarence Birdseye invents the process for quick freezing, making frozen food possible.

1924, January 25........ The first modern Winter Olympic Games are held in Chamonix, France.

1924, February 14 .... IBM Corporation is founded.

1924, Thanksgiving ..... The first Macy's Thanksgiving Day Parade is held in New York City.

1925, January 5........... Nellie Tayloe Ross becomes the first female governor in the United States, in Wyoming.

1925, June 13 .... Charles Francis Jenkins invents Radiovision, an early version of television.

1925, April .... F. Scott Fitzgerald publishes *The Great Gatsby*.

1925, May 5 .... John Scopes is arrested for teaching evolution and the "Monkey Trial" takes place.

1926, March 16 .... Robert Goddard demonstrates the first liquid-fueled rocket in Auburn, Massachusetts.

1926, May 9 .... Floyd Bennett and Richard Byrd complete the first flight to the North Pole and back.

1926, October .... Ernest Hemingway publishes *The Sun Also Rises*.

1926, November 15 ..... The NBC Radio Network is formed.

1927 .... Philo T. Farnsworth invents a complete television system, which will be patented three years later.

1927, April 22–May 5 .. The Great Mississippi Flood affects more than 700,000 people.

1927, May 21 .... Charles Lindbergh completes the first transatlantic flight and lands in Paris, France.

1927, August 10 .... Work begins on Mount Rushmore.

1927, August 23 .... Sacco and Vanzetti are executed.

1927, October 6 .... The first talking movie, *The Jazz Singer*, opens.

1928, June 17 .... Amelia Earhart becomes the first woman to fly over the Atlantic Ocean.

1928, August 27 .... The United States and 14 other nations sign the Kellogg-Briand Pact, "outlawing" war.

1928, November 6 ...... Herbert Hoover is elected president.

1928, November 18 ..... Mickey Mouse is introduced in the Walt Disney cartoon *Steamboat Willie*.

1928, December 21 ..... Congress approves the construction of the Boulder Dam, which will later be renamed the Hoover Dam.

1929, January 15 .... Martin Luther King Jr. is born in Atlanta, Georgia.

1929, February 14 .... The St. Valentine's Day Massacre takes place in Chicago. Al Capone's gang murders six members of the rival Bugs Moran gang.

1929, October 29 .... Black Friday, when the stock market crashes and the Great Depression begins.

Introduction

Why Were the Twenties "Roaring"?

Do you ever wonder why historians call the era of the 1920s in American history the "Roaring Twenties"?

The 1920s were nicknamed the Roaring Twenties because it was a time when everything seemed exciting and new and modern, when everything seemed to move faster than ever before.

1920s TIDBIT

The twenties "roared" because the mood of the country was one of prosperity, change, and innovation.

Do you think that we live in a period of time when things are changing? Maybe you remember a time before smartphones and tablet readers, Twitter and Facebook. A time when only astronauts could fly into outer space. Isn't it exciting to imagine the possibilities of the future, such as Google Glass and electric cars, and realize it's already here?

The years between World War I and the Great Depression were an era of excitement, movement, and a newer, faster pace of life. It was the beginning of modern life, modern inventions, and a kind of popular culture that Americans had never experienced before.

Radio and movies helped spread new trends in fashion, music, and behavior. The traditional lifestyles and values were changing. People had more money to spend and new consumer goods to spend it on. Women, especially young women, were breaking free from their old roles and finding that they could have more freedom to work as well as raise a family. It was a time of fresh air after the long, dark years of World War I.

THE GREAT WAR

World War I (1914–1918) was devastating to Americans and Europeans. In total, more people died than in any previous war: 9 million soldiers and 5 million civilians. Twenty-eight countries were involved in the war, and it cost more than $300 billion. It was the first time that new devices such as poison gas, airplanes, and long-range artillery had been used. Millions of men were left permanently disabled. It changed the governments and economies of many European countries and, as a result, the United States became a leading industrial and economic power on its own. After the war, Americans could concentrate more on their own country after so many years spent focused on the rest of the world.

Most Americans came out of World War I certain that there would never be another war as terrible as what they had just experienced. The overall feeling was one of optimism. As restrictions on consumer goods were lifted, most workers saw their wages increase by as much as 22 percent.

There is a lot of new vocabulary in this book! Turn to the glossary in the back when you come to a word you don't understand. Practice your new vocabulary in the VOCAB LAB activities in each chapter.

KEY IDEA

Use the QR codes throughout this book as takeoff points for further exploration. They suggest videos to view online and download. When a QR code is provided, you can use a smartphone or tablet app to access the suggestion directly.

Interested in primary sources? Look for this icon:

The years between 1900 and 1920 saw the start of a time of change in America, as the lifestyles and values left over from the end of the nineteenth century began to give way to new ways of living and seeing the world. Many people still lived in rural areas, but the movement of people into cities was increasing. Cars slowly became less expensive and more common.

Have you ever seen pictures of women in the early 1900s? Women dressed modestly, often in long skirts, and were mostly expected to stay at home to be housewives and mothers. But women began to enter the workforce in larger numbers as industry and factory jobs increased. With the advent of the "flapper"—the new, modern young woman with short skirts, short hair, and much more social freedom—women's roles began to change.

A TIME OF CHANGE

In *The Roaring Twenties: Discover the Era of Prohibition, Flappers, and Jazz*, you'll see that all of this transition served as the foundation of the Roaring Twenties. It was an era when everything seemed to change. As African Americans move out of the rural South to the cities, their jazz music inspired a musical transformation in America. As Prohibition outlawed the manufacture and sale of alcohol, gangsters and organized crime became commonplace. New inventions greatly altered everyday life.

From the roles that men and women played in society to the way they viewed money and spending, the 1920s was a bridge from the old ways of living to the modern world. You'll compare many aspects of the decade with today. And you might discover that many of the things we take for granted as part of modern American life got their start in this wild, exciting, often uncertain decade.

Chapter 1
We're In the Money

Why did so many people have more money to spend during the 1920s?

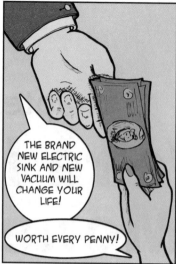

As wages increased and people and businesses made money in the stock market, their standard of living grew, creating more disposable income.

How many different items does your family buy in a year? More than one hundred? It's probably thousands. Today, the economy of the United States depends heavily on consumers. People see millions of products advertised in print, on television, and on the Internet. They can buy these products in many different stores or on many different websites online. They can pay with cash, checks, or credit cards, and pay for expensive goods such as cars and homes in installments during many years.

But it wasn't always like this. This kind of consumer economy got its start in the Roaring Twenties. It was more than just a combination of a growing economy and consumers with more money to spend. The discovery of the power of advertising by manufacturers and merchants—and the invention of so many new products to buy—changed everything.

LIVING IT UP

Most Americans saw their standard of living increase during the 1920s. The standard of living is the degree of wealth and material goods that is available to a person or a community. Wages increased, giving the average worker more money to spend. Can you imagine life without electricity, indoor plumbing, central heating, toasters, microwaves, and vacuum cleaners? All of these things, plus a wide range of other labor-saving appliances, became more available and more affordable for many households.

But what led to such a strong economy? One reason was industry's ability to manufacture and distribute goods on a larger scale than ever before. New technology that used oil and electricity in manufacturing made factories more productive and made it easier to produce huge amounts of goods. The emphasis was no longer on people handcrafting quality items one by one. Instead, goods were uniformly made by machine, allowing more of them to be made quickly. This is called mass production.

Mass production was possible because of innovations such as the assembly line, which was pioneered by Henry Ford. An assembly line made it much faster to build things such as automobiles. This kind of scientific management was used by businesses and factories all over the country. It is a concept based on applying science to manufacturing to find ways to produce goods more efficiently.

1920s TIDBIT

A famous World War I song asked, "How ya gonna keep 'em down on the farm, after they've seen Paree?" Soldiers had seen Paris and other great European cities. Many people were no longer as willing to live in isolated, rural communities after the war.

ASSEMBLY LINE MANUFACTURING

An assembly line is an arrangement of workers and tasks in a factory that is set up to make, or assemble, products as quickly as possible. Each worker in the line has his or her own task that he or she performs over and over again on product after product.

Antitrust laws make it difficult for one business to take over an entire industry, which is called a monopoly. When large corporations become monopolies, there is no competition among businesses. This leads to higher prices for the consumer.

The government also followed policies that encouraged big businesses to grow. These policies included tax cuts and not enforcing antitrust laws. Antitrust laws were designed to prevent large corporations from becoming monopolies, and to encourage free trade by allowing for competition among businesses.

Instead, the government looked the other way while corporations grew bigger and controlled more and more of their markets, swallowing up small rival companies. For example, by the year 1929, 85 percent of all cars sold were made by just three companies: Ford, General Motors, and Chrysler. These companies could also raise money by selling stocks and bonds, which meant that they needed fewer bank loans. As a result, banks shifted more of their attention to investing their funds in the stock market.

SILENT CAL

President Calvin Coolidge, whose presidency spanned much of the Roaring Twenties, was nicknamed "Silent Cal" because he was a quiet man when it came to conversation. This quietness seemed to spill over into his economic policies as well. Part of Coolidge's image was one of thrift and frugality.

PRODUCTS WITH STAYING POWER

It wasn't just big-ticket items that became popular in the 1920s. Do you recognize any of these products from your own food cabinet or refrigerator? Planter's Peanuts, Hires Root Beer, Kool-Aid drink mix, Kellogg's Corn Flakes, Peter Pan peanut butter, Cracker Jack, Dr. Pepper, Coca-Cola, and Kraft cheese all became available in the 1920s!

Coolidge was a Vermont farmer. Photographs of him working on his farm emphasized the traditional values of plain living, saving money, and not indulging in excessive spending. This attitude was at odds with the mood of the country of growing consumer spending, the proliferation of consumer goods, and rising wages. But it led to many money-saving policies in government.

Coolidge wanted to see the same thrift in government spending that he advocated in his personal lifestyle. He paid off the national debt and eliminated waste wherever possible. He also helped create a business environment in which advertising played a bigger role than ever before.

Coolidge disliked having government regulate business too much, and this is what helped the large corporations to grow. In an address to the American Society of Newspaper Editors in 1925, he said, "After all, the chief business of the American people is business. They are profoundly concerned with buying, selling, investing, and prospering in the world." Coolidge always supported business growth, and tried to make the government work like a business organization that was conscious of how much money it spent.

"There is no dignity quite so impressive, and no one independence quite so important, as living within your means."

—Calvin Coolidge

FIRST ON FILM

In February 1924, President Coolidge became the first president to make a public radio address. He was also the first president to appear in a presidential film with sound recording. Nearly a hundred years later, President Barack Obama became the first president to use social media such as Facebook and Twitter to reach the public. How might our different forms of media affect the way we think about presidents and other world leaders?

You can see Coolidge's film.

"JUST 24 EASY PAYMENTS . . ."

Consumer credit was another innovation that helped create a bustling consumer economy. American households could now afford to buy expensive items such as cars through credit, instead of having to save large amounts of cash to make purchases. The installment plan was a form of credit that suited families very well. Consumers could buy cars, furniture, refrigerators, jewelry, and many other products by paying a set amount of money every month during a period of years until the item was paid for. Of course, they also paid interest on that purchase. But financing was a way for families to have all the comforts they wanted right away.

By 1928, nearly 65 percent of all cars in the United States were purchased on credit. Americans in the 1920s did not worry about relying on credit, since they could not imagine a time when the economy might slow down. They could not imagine that monthly payments could become difficult to make. Does this sound familiar?

Journalist Samuel Strauss published many articles criticizing what he saw as an excessive focus on material goods, which he called "an empire of things." He also criticized department stores and the linking of holidays and shopping.

What really spurred consumer credit and borrowing was advertising. Businesses had always advertised their goods, but usually at a local level. A store might put ads in the local newspaper to advertise a product, but only people in the area would know about it.

Starting in the 1920s, advertising agencies began to run national print advertising campaigns. People all over the country, whether they lived in urban, suburban, or rural locations, all saw the same ads for the same goods. These ads told consumers that if they wanted to live the good life, they needed to have certain things, such as cars, vacuum cleaners, and the latest refrigerator. Everyone saw the same ads, which created a national culture. People on the West Coast and the East Coast and in the middle of America all wanted the same consumer goods.

This common culture was fed by movies, which exposed people to the same experiences. Radio was also an effective means for advertising new products, which people all over the country suddenly decided they had to buy.

The 1920s could be called the beginning of the advertising age.

A TRADITION IS BORN

The Macy's Thanksgiving Day Parade, which airs on television every year, actually got its start in 1924. The parade was a way to sell children's toys during the Christmas season. Today, the Macy's Thanksgiving Day Parade is an important tradition that marks the beginning of the Christmas season. Macy's employees participate in the preparation and the parade itself.

Through advertising, companies developed new methods to entice Americans to keep buying, even after they had accumulated many of the newest luxuries. Every year, companies marketed new products. These might be a new model of a car and newer, updated versions of existing products, such as washing machines. The products were marketed through advertising and public relations campaigns to convince consumers that they needed the latest and greatest version of a product if they were truly going to achieve the American dream.

Sales were helped by the growing number of catalog mail-order companies, as well as by chain and department stores such as the A&P grocery stores, Woolworth's, J.C. Penney, and Walgreen Drugs. These catalogs and stores made the same consumer goods easily available to people all over the country. The widespread use of automobiles also made it possible for more people to travel to nearby towns and buy goods in stores.

Of course, not everyone in 1920s America was comfortable with this new, modern life and consumer culture. In particular, there was conflict between those who lived in urban, modern, consumer-driven areas and those who lived in small towns in rural parts of the country. Those who did not live in cities often felt that the new, modern values were threatening their traditional way of life. Have you noticed that the tension between traditional and modern values is still a topic of conversation in American life?

PLAYING THE MARKET

The 1920s were a time when the attitude toward the stock market changed. The stock market is the place where stocks and bonds are bought and sold. Stocks are units of ownership in a company, tiny pieces of a company that belong to the stock owner. The goal of buying stock is to hold onto it until it can be sold for more than the buyer originally paid for it, to make a profit. However, if the company does badly, the stock price falls. Then the stock owner loses money.

Before the Roaring Twenties, people saw the stock market as a place for long-term investment. Those who held onto stocks during a long period of time were usually the most successful. But this changed as people began to think of the market as a place to get rich quickly. Stories of people becoming millionaires were common, and people began to trade stock tips feverishly. As more people bought stocks, stock prices continued to rise, which fueled even more buying.

Not everyone had the cash to buy stocks, but in a new, credit-based society, they could buy stocks on margin. This means that instead of paying full price for stocks at the time of purchase, the buyer puts down 10 to 20 percent of the purchase price and borrows the rest from the stockbroker. How could this be risky? If the price of the stock falls below the amount of the loan, the broker can issue a margin call. This means the buyer has to repay the loan immediately, in cash. But as stocks kept going up and up during the 1920s, it didn't seem as though there was an end in sight to this stock boom. People continued to take the risk and buy on margin.

1920s TIDBIT

Walgreens Pharmacy opened in 1901 and is still thriving more than a hundred years later. You may have visited one! In 1922 the shops first served malted milkshakes at their soda fountain counters, which became one of the famous treats of the twenties.

BANKS BUY IN

It seemed so easy to make money in the stock market that companies began placing money in the market as well. Some banks even put their customers' money into stocks, usually without telling them. But throughout the 1920s, there didn't seem to be any reason to worry. Times were good and almost everyone felt excited about the economy.

NO FUN FOR ME

Farmers in the 1920s were under heavy amounts of debt. Between 1920 and 1932, one in four American farms had to be sold because of debt. Those farmers often moved to urban areas, looking for work.

Farmers, African Americans, and immigrants were three groups of people who did not share in the overall prosperity of the Roaring Twenties. Even though one-fifth of the U.S. population made its living from farming, most farmers were struggling financially and did not have electricity or telephones. Because of new farming technology, farmers were producing more crops than ever before, but the surpluses of these crops resulted in falling prices.

African Americans often lived in poverty in the South. They had a lower standard of living and fewer opportunities. The falling price of cotton made it even more difficult to make a living from farming. Many families migrated north to cities. This had begun during the labor shortages of World War I, when so many men were fighting in Europe that there weren't enough left to work in all the jobs at home. African Americans moved to find work, as well as to escape racism and racial violence. Many were lured by industries that needed inexpensive labor, but they found themselves competing with whites and immigrants for jobs.

Immigrants suffered from restrictive laws that limited the number of people from certain areas who were allowed to immigrate to the United States. There was also a general hostility toward them that made it difficult to find any job, let alone one that paid well.

CREDIT, THEN AND NOW

The 1920s saw the birth of consumer credit, with charge accounts at stores, credit cards, and installment loans. Today it's hard to imagine modern life without these kinds of credit. Yet in both eras, families often found themselves in severe financial hardship due to overusing easy credit and then not being able to pay their bills.

- **Create a graph that compares consumer credit from the 1920s through today.** You can research just one type of credit, such as installment loans for purchasing automobiles, or the use of credit cards, which in the 1920s were mostly used for gasoline companies and hotels. On your graph, decide how to organize your information so that you can show the year and the number of people who have a credit card or an installment loan.

- **Analyze your data.** From events such as the stock market crash in 1929, the Great Depression in the 1930s, and the economic downturns of the early 2000s, what conclusions can you draw about consumer credit during these times?

- **Create a second graph showing modern credit card use.** Use the data for each year from 1950 (the advent of credit cards such as MasterCard and Visa) through today. What's the average consumer's credit card debt? What trends can you see? Is credit card debt steadily growing or does it rise and fall?

To investigate more, consider the fact that credit card companies are now targeting college students as potential users, often before they even have a steady income. Do you think this is a way to help students build good, responsible credit or a potential trap for overspending?

Inquire & Investigate

VOCAB LAB

Write down what you think each word means: **economy**, **mass production**, **monopoly**, **stock**, **proliferation**, **consumer goods**, **thrift**, and **financing**.

Compare your definitions with those of your friends or classmates. Did you all come up with the same meanings? Turn to the text and glossary if you need help.

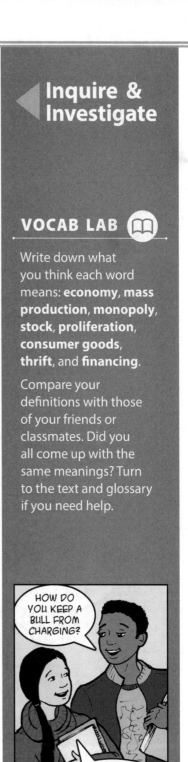

HOW DO YOU KEEP A BULL FROM CHARGING?

TAKE AWAY HIS CREDIT CARDS!

Despite the overall
image of the 1920s as
a time when everyone
enjoyed prosperity and
a better standard of
living, it was actually
a time when the gap
between the rich and
the poor increased.
Not everyone was "in
the money," and not
everyone was excited
and optimistic.

THE STOCK MARKET

During the 1920s, everyone seemed to be interested in playing the stock market. People traded tips about the best stock to buy, and when to buy or sell in order to make the most money. Here's your chance to try your own stock market investing, but without the risk of losing any money.

- **You have $100 to spend.** Your goal is to make as much money as you can. Do you want to invest your money in the stock market, put it into a savings account, or divide it between both options?

- **Research several companies that you've heard of or are interested in.** What do you think might be a good investment based on economic conditions and popularity? Are there any trends you should consider? For example, if you think that organic foods are going to become more and more popular, then research stock in an organic food distributing company.

- **Check with several local banks and find out what interest rates they pay on a traditional savings account.** If you leave some or all of your $100 in that account for a month, how much interest will you earn?

- **Based on your research into company stock prices and savings account interest rates, decide how to invest your $100.** You can put it all in stocks or all in savings, or split it between the two. Can you create a chart that shows the price you "paid" when you purchased that stock, and then track the stock's price every day for a month on your chart?

- **At the end of a month, calculate how much money your stocks and savings have made.** For example, if you bought five shares in Company X at $20 a share, and the price after a month is $22, then you could sell your stock and make a profit of $10. How does this compare with the amount of interest you've earned on your savings account? Can you graph the ups and downs of your stock price and your savings to visually compare their growth?

To investigate more, follow stock prices through a period of several weeks or months. Note if there is something such as a natural disaster, an economic crisis, or a sudden surge of interest in your company that drives its stock prices up or down. What trends do you see? Can you relate the rising or falling of the stock market to any particular events in the news or around the world?

ADVERTISING ON THE RADIO

The growing popularity of radio in the 1920s meant that companies could advertise across the sound waves. People all over the country would hear about their products.

Radio advertisements were much different from ads found in newspapers and magazines, and extremely different from today's visual ads on television and the Internet. Description was more important, since the product couldn't be shown, and actors' voices had to convey emotion and enthusiasm, since their faces could not be seen.

• **Research a product that was widely available in the 1920s, such as a new food item, a style of clothing, or a medicine or beauty product.** What does it look like? Smell like? Taste like? What are the selling points that might make someone want to buy it? Will it make the buyer's life easier? Better?

1920s TIDBIT

The Curtiss Candy Company promoted its new Baby Ruth candy bar by parachuting free bars into the streets of Pittsburgh, Pennsylvania, from an airplane.

- **Research radio advertising from the 1920s.** You'll find examples of vintage ads online that you can listen to. You can also listen to ads on current radio stations. What makes them appealing or not? What makes you want to try the product?

- **Write a radio script for the item you've researched.** This script is what your radio ad will say. Remember that you have to tell your listeners what it is, what it does, and why they would want to buy it. What cues do the actors need so they know what emotions to convey in the script? Will you use music or sound effects?

- **Once you've written your script, make a recording of your advertisement, either by yourself or with the help of several friends.** Then play your advertisement for your class or your family. Did the ad make them curious about the product? Would they buy it and give it a try? Why or why not? Overall, did they find your advertisement to be convincing?

- **If your product is not a brand that's still familiar today (such as Jell-O), research if the product is still available.** If not, when did it disappear from American store shelves? Can you discover why it might not have lasted?

To investigate more, listen to ads on the radio today and compare them to television or Internet ads. Does the radio still rely on methods such as musical jingles, sound effects, or celebrity voices? How do they make up for not having a visual aspect? Are they ever more effective than television ads? Do television ads use any of the same methods as radio?

Inquire & Investigate

BUYER BEWARE

Because the economy grew so quickly in the 1920s, it also saw the creation of many consumer protection organizations. The Truth in Advertising movement was created by industries themselves to make sure that advertising was truthful and ethical. Advertising shouldn't lie or go against accepted rules of behavior. Other movements emphasized educating consumers about home ownership, thrift and saving, and unfair advertising and pricing.

Check out these vintage radios and print ads.

LET'S TALK WITH PRESIDENT COOLIDGE

You are a journalist in the 1920s, and you have a chance to interview President Calvin Coolidge on his farm in Vermont. President Coolidge is known for his views on thrift and for living the simple life, even though he was president at a time when people felt they had more money to spend than in the past and more new and exciting inventions to spend it on.

- **Research President Coolidge's life, his farm, and his opinions on money and the economy while he was president.** How would you write an interview with President Coolidge from the perspective of a journalist who writes for a magazine read mostly by conservative, rural families? Would these families still follow traditional values such as thrift, saving, and careful spending? How does the president's lifestyle on his farm embody these values?

- **Write another interview as a journalist working for a flashy, modern magazine read by younger city dwellers.** Are these readers more likely to be actively involved in the new, roaring lifestyle, interested in the latest consumer goods, and eager to invest in the stock market for quick wealth? How can you make President Coolidge's views on thrift and conservative living appeal to this kind of reader?

To investigate more, find examples of interviews of a more current political figure, such as President Barack Obama or Senator Marco Rubio, written from two very different perspectives, such as a conservative magazine and a magazine intended for more liberal readers. What differences are there between the interviews?

Chapter 2
Politics and Prohibition

Why was Prohibition
such a major issue
during the 1920s?

Prohibition not only changed American culture during the 1920s, it also led to more organized crime.

The Roaring Twenties was a time when many people were enjoying a higher income, more consumer goods, and more freedom. But it was also a time when the country faced serious political issues. After the horrors of World War I, America wanted to isolate itself from the rest of the world and focus on patriotism and domestic issues. And there were plenty of domestic issues to struggle with, from Prohibition to the Ku Klux Klan to the Red Scare. And yet, the United States could not completely close itself off from the rest of the globe.

PROHIBITION

On January 16, 1919, the 18th Amendment to the Constitution of the United States was ratified. The amendment took effect one year later, on January 17, 1920.

The amendment read:

Section 1 After one year from the ratification of this article the manufacture, sale, or transportation of intoxicating liquors within, the importation thereof into, or the exportation thereof from the United States and all territory subject to the jurisdiction thereof for beverage purposes is hereby prohibited.

Section 2 The Congress and the several States shall have concurrent power to enforce this article by appropriate legislation.

Section 3 This article shall be inoperative unless it shall have been ratified as an amendment to the Constitution by the legislatures of the several States, as provided in the Constitution, within seven years from the date of the submission hereof to the States by the Congress.

The 18th Amendment was the first constitutional amendment that actually gave a date by which it had to be ratified or else it would be discarded. However, at the time, many states were already following a version of Prohibition that had come from the work of temperance groups.

These groups included the American Temperance Society and the Women's Christian Temperance Union, which were first started in the 1820s to convince people to stop drinking and also to improve public morals. These powerful groups included church communities, business leaders, feminists, and political reformers. They wanted to ban alcohol because of the effects alcoholism had on family life, morality, traditional values, and individual health. Women in particular supported the temperance movement because too many men spent all their money on alcohol, leaving nothing for their families for food. Even factory owners supported temperance as a way to keep their workers productive.

"Our country has deliberately undertaken a great social and economic experiment, noble in motive and far-reaching in purpose."

—Herbert Hoover, president of the United States from 1929 to 1933, talking about Prohibition, which is often referred to as the Great Experiment after Hoover's quote

Some temperance groups tried to have the Bible rewritten to delete any mention of alcohol.

Since wives were still expected to stay at home and care for their children rather than get jobs, families often relied solely on the husbands' paychecks for food and housing.

Politicians did not want to alienate these groups. Even though many senators were reluctant to vote for Prohibition, they also did not want to go on record as voting against it. As a result of this and many years of work by the temperance movement, the 18th Amendment received its required three-fourths approval from the states and was ratified just a year after its introduction.

The alcohol industry, however, was given a year before the amendment was to be implemented. Knowing that Prohibition would take a heavy toll, the government gave the industry the extra year to give it time to adjust to the upcoming restriction.

THE VOLSTEAD ACT

Many people think that Prohibition prohibited the drinking of alcohol. It actually only prohibited the "manufacture, sale, or transportation" of alcohol. In order to enforce the new amendment, Congress passed a bill on January 17, 1920, called the Volstead Act.

The act defined an alcoholic beverage as anything containing more than 0.5 percent alcohol, and also included beer and wine in the ban. **The Volstead Act read, in part:**

> No one shall manufacture, sell, purchase, transport, or prescribe any liquor without first obtaining a permit from the commissioner so to do, except that a person may, without a permit, purchase and use liquor for medicinal purposes when prescribed by a physician.

At first, it seemed as though the 18th Amendment was working. The amount of liquor consumed in the United States fell by as much as 50 percent, there were fewer arrests for drunkenness, and illegal liquor became so expensive that the average person could not afford it. However, there were people who never paid attention to Prohibition. Many became very good at outwitting the Prohibition enforcement agents.

NOT THE SAME FOR EVERYONE

Prohibition deepened the divide between the urban and rural populations. Statistics from 1924 showed that while 95 percent of the citizens of Kansas were obeying Prohibition, only 5 percent of people who lived in New York State did.

1920s TIDBIT

"Cruises to nowhere" were boat trips to international waters, where it was legal to serve alcohol. Usually these boats cruised in circles while passengers had parties.

In 1925, it is estimated that there were anywhere from 30,000 to 100,000 speakeasies in just New York City.

1920s TIDBIT

The soft drink industry benefitted enormously from Prohibition. More people bought soda to hide the taste of illegal alcohol.

SPEAKEASIES

How did people manage to find alcohol when selling it was made illegal by a constitutional amendment? Most elected officials didn't try very hard to follow the law, and citizens didn't try either. People took advantage of the Volstead Act loophole and found doctors who would prescribe alcohol for "medical conditions."

Others manufactured their own alcohol, such as "bathtub gin," which was distilled and fermented in home bathtubs. Much of this homemade alcohol tasted awful and was dangerous, using ingredients such as grain alcohol with various flavorings such as juniper berries. When the alcohol used was denatured alcohol, a form of ethanol that is actually poisonous, it often killed those who drank it. Other dangerous ingredients used to make alcoholic beverages were camphor, embalming fluid, mercury, and jake, which is an extract of Jamaican ginger that can cause paralysis and death. Some people also made their own liquor using homemade stills, fermenting grains such as corn or barley into a mash and then heating it to condense the alcohol.

HE STARTED WITH BATHTUB GIN...

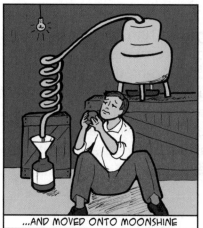

...AND MOVED ONTO MOONSHINE

...IF HE WAS LUCKY, FROM THE DOC.

Many people, especially in urban areas, were able to get alcohol in speakeasies. These were nightclubs that operated in secret, often in rundown buildings or behind doors where the customers had to give a password in order to be admitted. The term "speakeasy" supposedly comes from the fact that the customers had to "speak easy" (remain quiet) so that the club would not be found by law enforcement officials. However, many speakeasies routinely included police officers and city officials among their customers.

BOOTLEGGING

Another unexpected result of Prohibition was a rise in the role of organized crime. Bootleggers were people who made and sold alcohol illegally, and they could make a great deal of money during this time. As a result, much of the bootlegging business was taken over by gangsters. Al Capone's gang ruled Chicago, the American Mafia operated in cities such as Chicago and New York, and the Purple Gang covered Detroit.

STEALING SIPS

People who wanted access to alcohol also developed clever ways of carrying it undetected. A flask is a small container for secretly carrying alcohol. Some methods used included hip flasks, canes that were hollow and made to hold liquid, false books that concealed flasks, and flasks that could be hidden in garters under women's clothing.

These gangster bootlegging organizations, which were also involved in other kinds of crime, prompted frequent violence. Rival gangs engaged in turf wars and shoot-outs in the streets or assassinated key members of other gangs.

In Chicago alone, authorities reported as many as 400 gang-related murders every year. Because many law enforcement officials and city leaders were being bribed, threatened, or paid off by these gangsters, the gangs were able to operate outside of the law for the most part. Political corruption was widespread.

One of the worst incidents of gang violence was the St. Valentine's Day Massacre in Chicago in 1929, which was blamed on Al Capone. Seven men were killed in a fight about who controlled the liquor business.

THE KLAN RISES AGAIN

As much as Prohibition affected the entire nation, it was not the only political and social issue that Americans were facing at the time. The Ku Klux Klan started in the years following the Civil War as a protest against Reconstruction. It had faded out in the late nineteenth century, but had come back to life in 1915.

By 1923, nationwide membership was approaching 1 million. The Klan was promoting itself as a representation of good morals, fundamentalist religion, and patriotism. Members supported traditional family values and were against the new, modern life, including jazz, movies, and divorce. But the Klan was best known for its prejudice against blacks and immigrants and for being anti-Catholic and anti-Semitic. This message of racism and intolerance was accepted by many people, especially in rural America, who felt threatened by the changes in society that were taking places in the 1920s.

The Klan was not just a group for poor, uneducated Americans. In the 1920s, the Klan included many respectable, middle-class Americans who owned homes and made good livings.

While the Klan would be known for more violent racial intolerance during the Civil Rights era of the 1950s and 1960s, during the Roaring Twenties it was a milder group. Many Americans, especially those who believed modern life was sweeping away all the traditional values that were important to them, felt at home in this group.

By the end of the twenties, though, the popularity of the Klan fell as stories of corruption, lawlessness, tax evasion, and other scandals came to light. Membership dwindled. And yet one aspect of the Klan's prejudice—being against foreigners and immigration—was a reflection of a fear that was sweeping the entire country: the Red Scare.

KKK BEHAVIOR

Ku Klux Klan members were known for wearing white robes and masks. Their acts of violence included burning crosses on the lawns of people whose affiliations or behavior the Klan didn't like. The Klan was also known for beatings, tar and feathering, kidnappings, mutilations, and even killings. At the same time, however, the Klan of the 1920s tried to maintain a more community-friendly image.

SEEING RED

UNREST IN RUSSIA

During the Russian Revolution in 1917, the Russian Social Democratic Workers' Party took over the country's royal government. It captured and executed the entire royal family of Tsar Nicholas II. The Workers' Party objected to what it saw as an unequal distribution of resources such as food, shelter, and money among the rich and the poor. A few months later, the Bolsheviks, led by Vladimir Lenin, overthrew the temporary government of the Russian Social Democratic Workers' Party because they wanted to end Russia's engagement in World War I. Their vision was of a country ruled by the people who worked the hardest, and their methods were often violent. The Bolsheviks became the Communist Party in 1918.

After the Bolshevik Revolution took place in Russia in 1917, a communist party was established in the United States. Communism was a system based on the belief that property and goods belonged to the state, and that people should share them. It was an idea that threatened the capitalism and new consumer culture of the United States. Most people in the United States did not want to live under communism.

By 1920, many people had began to fear the influence of communists, who were called "reds" for the red flag of the international communist organization. This fear created an atmosphere of distrust against anyone who didn't seem to be a loyal American. Many Americans feared that the influx of immigrants, many from Eastern European countries, would result in a communist takeover of their country.

In addition to fearing communists, Americans also found reason to fear anarchists. These people didn't believe in any form of government at all. They were known to use violent bombings targeted at government officials and institutions.

Many patriotic Americans reacted to communists and anarchists with suspicion and fear, and the Red Scare was born. U.S. Attorney General A. Mitchell Palmer received permission to set up an anti-radical division of the U.S. Department of Justice, and he began rounding up suspected anarchists and other radicals. People were held without warrants in overcrowded, unheated jails.

AS SACCO AND VANZETTI WERE TRIED – COUNTLESS OTHERS WERE WAITING...

Freedom of speech was restricted during this time because people were afraid to even talk about communism and other radical ideas. They didn't want to be accused of belonging to one of those groups.

The Red Scare culminated in the trial of Ferdinando Nicola Sacco and Bartolomeo Vanzetti in 1921. These two men, who were Italian immigrants and anarchists, were charged with the murder of a Massachusetts paymaster and his bodyguard. A paymaster is a person in charge of paying wages. Despite flimsy evidence, they were convicted by a jury that was prejudiced against them because they were immigrants, anarchists, and had participated in organizing labor strikes. The two men were sent to the electric chair in 1927.

"Never in our full life could we hope to do such work for tolerance, for justice, for man's understanding of man as now we do by accident."

—Bartolomeo Vanzetti said this to a reporter shortly before he and Sacco were executed. What do you think he means by this statement?

Every major capital city, including Paris, London, and even as far away as Tokyo, Sydney, and Johannesburg, saw protests over the conviction and execution of Sacco and Vanzetti.

ISOLATIONISM VS. LEAGUE OF NATIONS

With WWI still fresh in their minds, U.S. politicians wanted to maintain their position of isolationism. They did not want to get pulled into another war simply because of the country's membership in the League of Nations.

A PATRIOTIC NATION

The Red Scare only increased the distrust and resentment that many Americans felt about immigrants. After World War I, many Americans were isolationists. These are people who wanted to keep America to itself, not participate in more foreign wars or political incidents, and restrict the number of immigrants who could come to their country. Congress passed the Emergency Quota Act of 1921, and then the Immigration Act of 1924, both of which drastically limited the number of immigrants allowed into the country.

The disillusionment of the country following World War I influenced foreign policy. President Warren G. Harding refused to join the League of Nations in 1919. The League—the predecessor to the United Nations— was an organization that was intended to prevent future wars through disarmament. It worked to settle international disputes through arbitration and negotiation. League of Nations members also wanted to address human rights issues, such as global health and the protection of minorities. Global health is the health of all populations in the world.

Harding and the U.S. Senate refused to join the League of Nations because of one section in the agreement. That section bound the United States to assist any other League of Nations member if it was attacked.

The United States did participate in several antiwar treaties, such as the Five-Power Naval Treaty of 1922. This treaty prevented the Americans and British from fortifying their bases in the Far East. At the Washington Disarmament Conference of 1921–1922, which all world navy powers attended, participants agreed to a 10-year halt on the construction of new battleships as a way to slow the naval arms race.

Because of World War I, many Americans became pacifists and worked in antiwar movements. They sent an antiwar petition with 2 million signatures to the government in Washington, D.C. asking it to outlaw war. President Calvin Coolidge and Secretary of State Frank B. Kellogg agreed to meet with French Minister of Foreign Affairs Aristide Briand. The French proposed a peace pact in which both nations agreed never to go to war against each other. Soon, other nations agreed to join the pact, and on August 27, 1928, 15 nations signed the Kellogg-Briand Pact in Paris. Later, another 47 nations joined in, and the U.S. Senate ratified the agreement.

The 1920s unfolded as a time of both cultural and political issues. But while Americans worried about these ongoing changes, they were also amazed and excited by a constant stream of new inventions that were changing the way they lived.

BROKEN PROMISES

The Kellogg-Briand Pact did not succeed in keeping the world at peace. In fact, plenty of wars have broken out among its member countries since the pact was signed. However, it did provide an important legal basis for trying and sentencing the people responsible for acts of war.

1920s TIDBIT

In 1924, Congress passed an act that officially made all Native Americans citizens of the United States. Before that, only certain tribes under certain treaties had been granted citizenship.

ON THE JURY

It is 1921, and you are a juror on the robbery and murder trial of Nicola Sacco and Bartolomeo Vanzetti trial. Read about their supposed crimes and the evidence brought against them in court. How would you vote if you were on the jury: guilty or innocent? Defend your decision with specific facts and evidence from the case.

Evidence and facts to consider:

- **A cap with a hole in it picked up at the crime scene resembled one owned by Sacco.** Sacco denied ever owning the cap, or any cap with ear flaps.

- **One of the recovered bullets could not have been fired from Sacco's Colt automatic.** However, ballistics expert Proctor testified that "Bullet 3" was "consistent with being fired through [Sacco's] pistol."

- Several witnesses placed Sacco near the location of the crime around the time it was committed. None of the seven eyewitnesses was at all times certain of his or her identification. No one claimed to have seen Vanzetti during the actual shooting.

- Sacco was absent from his job at the 3-K shoe factory on the day of the crime. Sacco claimed to have been in Boston trying to get a passport from the Italian consulate.

- The gun found on Vanzetti at the time of his arrest resembled one that the paymaster's bodyguard was thought to be carrying at the time he was shot. Vanzetti testified that he bought the gun from a friend.

- In 1918 Sacco and Vanzetti had written for and donated money to an anarchist newspaper.

- In 1919 a circular attributed to "The American Anarchists" appeared throughout New England. In it, the American Anarchists, presumably the Italian-American Anarchists, threaten to "dynamite" officials in retaliation for the ongoing deportations and repression the anarchists are enduring.

- In 1919, in a round of bombings, Carlo Valdinoci (who had been in Mexico with Sacco and Vanzetti two years earlier) blew himself up outside the home of U.S. Attorney General Palmer. Sacco and Vanzetti were rumored to have taken part in the bombing.

Listen to the folk song by Joan Baez about Sacco and Vanzetti, which uses Vanzetti's own words written in a letter to his father. Does the song make you feel differently about the trial? Why would a folk singer from the 1970s be inspired by the story?

Inquire & Investigate

VOCAB LAB

Write down what you think each word means: **prohibition**, **patriotism**, **racism**, **isolate**, **ratify**, **temperance**, **speakeasy**, **corruption**, **communism**, **capitalism**, **disillusionment**, and **pacifist**.

Compare your definitions with those of your friends or classmates. Did you all come up with the same meanings? Turn to the text and glossary if you need help.

Inquire & Investigate

"When I sell liquor, it's bootlegging. When my patrons serve it on a silver tray on Lakeshore Drive [a wealthy section of Chicago], it's hospitality."

— Al Capone, commenting on the corruption surrounding the enforcement of Prohibition

THE GREAT DEBATE

Prohibition was responsible for many changes in society in the 1920s, both good and bad. While many people found it inconvenient or simply ignored it, others felt it decreased alcohol consumption and brought positive changes.

Here's your chance to debate Prohibition. The following is a list of PRO and CON character roles for the issue of Prohibition. In a classroom setting, each student can choose a role, research his or her position, and then divide into PRO and CON teams and debate each stance. The rest of the class decides which side has won the debate.

To do this activity on your own, write a paragraph for each character stating what his or her argument would be, for or against Prohibition. Follow the debate flow chart to organize your thoughts and ideas. Can you decide which side of the issue seems to have the most convincing set of arguments?

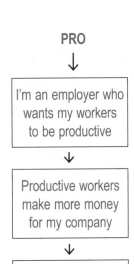

PRO	CON
↓	↓
I'm an employer who wants my workers to be productive	I'm a flapper who appreciates independence
↓	↓
Productive workers make more money for my company	I should be able to choose what I eat and drink
↓	↓
Employees who don't drink are more likely to get promotions	Prohibition takes away my rights as a modern woman

PRO Roles:

1. a government official upholding the law
2. a member of a temperance group
3. an employer
4. a gangster making money from bootlegging

CON Roles:

1. a gangster caught up in violent turf wars over bootlegging
2. a journalist who can see how alcohol is still available, despite the amendment
3. a flapper who likes to visit nightclubs and enjoy a drink
4. a bartender

To investigate more, can you think about what issue in the news today could be debated in a similar way?

THE UNTOUCHABLES

One of the most famous government crusaders against Al Capone and his bootlegging empire was Eliot Ness, who was a member of the Bureau of Prohibition. He assembled a team of men known as the Untouchables to enforce Prohibition in Chicago through raids on illegal stills and breweries. However, Capone was ultimately arrested and prosecuted for income tax evasion, not bootlegging.

AN EYEWITNESS SPEAKS

Prohibition sparked intense competition and violence between rival gangs. Research the St. Valentine's Day Massacre, which took place on February 14, 1929, between Al Capone and the rival Moran gang in Chicago. Then write two one-paragraph newspaper articles about the incident.

- **One newspaper article should describe what happened through the eyes of a reporter who is anti-gang.** How can this article use the incident to show how gang activity needs to be shut down?

- **The second article should be from the perspective of a reporter who is afraid to be too negative.** Why would this be the case? Maybe because he's being paid by Capone? Is he afraid to antagonize the crime boss too much?

- **Which article is more difficult to write?** Which one has a more convincing perspective?

SEEING RED

Read the original *New York Times* article about the St. Valentine's Day Massacre.

What's different about this newspaper article compared to articles written about violence today? What sounds similar? Do you think the author of the article had an opinion about the incident? Why?

To investigate more, consider that most big cities still have gang activity, often centered on drug trafficking instead of liquor. What similarities and differences are there between the gangs of today and the gangs of the 1920s?

Chapter 3

An Age of Invention

Why were new inventions so important to life in the 1920s?

The Roaring Twenties were more than just a gateway to modern life and a time of grappling with issues such as Prohibition. They also "roared" with the sounds of new inventions: car and airplane motors, rumbling machinery, and the sound of household appliances that saved women time and work. It was an age of invention.

HITTING THE ROAD

One invention that really became popular was the automobile. Thanks to cars, many other things were able to take place, such as families moving to the suburbs, shopping in central towns, traveling, and experiencing leisure activities such as going to the movies.

Automobiles weren't invented in the 1920s. They had been around for much longer than that. But it was a particular invention—having to do with manufacturing cars—that changed them into something that the average family could afford.

The new inventions and technologies of the 1920s changed American life more than at any other time. They made it possible to travel, receive news and entertainment, and enjoy more leisure time.

In 1900, which was the first year the U.S. Department of Commerce began keeping records on automobile ownership, there were only 8,000 cars in the entire country. Most of these cars were owned by wealthy people. When Henry Ford established his Ford Motor Company in 1903, there were 23,000 cars in the United States, but roads were still rough and better suited to horses and wagons. These numbers changed rapidly when, five years later, Ford introduced the Model T, an inexpensive car that many Americans could afford. The number of car owners jumped to 194,000. By 1918, Americans owned more than 5.5 million cars.

Why was Ford able to produce a less-expensive car that more people could afford? The answer was the assembly line. Instead of one person building a car from start to finish, Ford divided up the necessary tasks. Workers were given specific jobs to perform, such as tightening a certain sequence of bolts or installing a steering wheel. Ford broke up the car-building process into 84 steps, with each worker trained to do just one of these steps. Then Ford created a moving line on which the cars traveled from station to station, so that each worker performed his particular task on each car that moved past.

How did this speed up the process of building a car and save labor costs? The assembly line brought the work to the workers instead of having them move around, which saved time. The assembly line technique allowed Ford to reduce the price of a Model T from $850 in 1908 to just $360 in 1916. By 1925, a new Ford car rolled off the assembly line every 24 seconds.

On the Road

As cars became more common in American society, they not only changed peoples' lifestyles, but also the way that society functioned. With cars, people could move out of the cities to places where it was more pleasant to live and commute to their jobs. Of course, living in the suburbs made a car a necessity, and not just a luxury.

In 2007 there were an estimated 254 million passenger vehicles in the United States. What changes in our society and culture are related to this increase in the number of cars?

Ford instituted an installment credit plan that made it even easier for families to afford cars. Buyers paid a certain amount of money each month until they owned their automobiles. This is an example of how consumer credit helped the economy grow.

 **TIDBIT**

The assembly line technique was adopted by many other industries as well, speeding up production and helping to fuel mass consumption. In some ways, the 1920s were a second Industrial Revolution, a time when factories and manufacturers were able to increase production greatly by using new methods and taking advantage of electricity and other improved power sources.

The rise in the number of cars in America also affected the oil and rubber industries, which grew to produce enough gasoline and tires. Existing roads were improved and new roads constructed for the increasing automobile traffic. Trucks could now carry crops and perishable foods much more quickly, improving the quality and variety of food available for consumers to purchase. The growth in reliance on cars and trucks caused a drop in the use of railroads for transportation. The car was here to stay, and by 1930, almost one in three Americans owned one.

GOING UP

Cities changed as well during the 1920s. While many workers left cities to commute from suburban homes, many more Americans were moving to cities from poor, rural areas. For the first time in history, more people lived in cities than out in the country. Immigrants from other countries also swelled the populations of cities, as did African Americans who came from the rural South in search of better job opportunities.

As cities grew and companies required more office space, another modern invention became more important. The term "skyscraper" originally referred to a building that was 10 to 20 stories tall. But with improved construction methods, skyscrapers began reaching heights of 50 stories or more. Steel framing, concrete, elevators, and better plumbing and heating systems allowed builders to build higher and higher. Since city land was expensive in the 1920s, real estate developers wanted taller buildings that created more rentable space on one plot of land. Construction of the Empire State Building in New York City began in 1929, and the 102-story skyscraper was completed two years later.

Taller skyscrapers in cities such as New York and Chicago brought with them fears that the height of these buildings would impact another exciting technology of the 1920s: the airplane. Would these taller and taller towers become hazards for pilots flying over these cities?

TECHNOLOGY IN THE HOME

What were some of the home appliances that became popular in the 1920s? Toasters, coffee percolators, better refrigerators, and electric stoves made life easier in the kitchen. Washing machines, sewing machines, and irons made it easier to care for clothes. In addition to radios there were also gramophones and record players. Power saws, drills, and lathes made woodworking more efficient as well.

"**Charles Lindbergh flew like a poem into the heart of America.**"

—*The Springfield Republican* **newspaper**

As with automobiles, airplanes were invented well before the 1920s. The Wright brothers flew their first airplane in 1903, and during World War I planes were used for both fighting and reconnaissance. By 1923, airplanes were carrying passengers across the English Channel and the U.S. postal service was using airmail to carry mail across the country. But because flying was expensive and planes could not carry very many passengers at once, it wasn't really seen as a very efficient way to transport people . . . until 1927, when a young man named Charles Lindbergh sparked an interest in aviation.

Lindbergh flew airplanes as a stunt pilot and airmail carrier in the early 1920s. A man named Raymond Orteig offered a prize of $25,000 to the first person to fly the 3,600 miles (5,794 kilometers) from New York City to Paris nonstop, and Lindbergh accepted the challenge.

1920s TIDBIT

Raymond Orteig had first made his $25,000 offer in 1919. Several people tried to make the transatlantic flight from New York City to Paris and failed. Only a month before Lindbergh's success, one team crashed, killing both pilots, and another team was lost at sea.

On May 20, 1927, he took off from New York, arriving in Paris 33½ hours later, on May 21. Lindbergh's flight made him a national hero. It also brought about a new national interest in planes and flying.

Applications for pilot's licenses went up by 300 percent that year, and new airline companies were created, including United Airlines, American Airlines, and Trans-World Airlines. New planes carried 12 to 15 passengers at a time, instead of just one or two, and by the spring of 1929 there were 61 passenger airlines and 47 airmail companies. The age of flight was well under way.

ON THE AIR AND ON FILM

Many Americans heard about Lindbergh's flight on the radio or saw newsreels about it when they went to the movies. These two forms of entertainment were also inventions that became more widespread in the 1920s and heavily influenced popular culture.

GUESS MY WEIGHT

One reason Lindbergh's plane succeeded where others failed was because of its weight. The plane, engine, and pilot weighed 2,500 pounds (1,133 kilograms), but the fuel needed for a 3,600-mile flight (5,794 kilometers) weighed another 2,700 pounds (1,224 kilograms)! Lindbergh decided to fly without a co-pilot to keep the weight down, even though 33 hours alone in a plane was a daunting prospect.

National radio programming and advertising campaigns brought a common American culture to people all over the country.

By 1922, there were 600 radio stations all across the country, and 60 percent of American families had purchased radios by the end of the decade. People were no longer limited to news from just their area. They could experience a wider world, instant news bulletins, and the same entertainment programs as listeners in other states. Specific radio stations could create a feeling of community among certain listeners by creating their programs for groups such as farmers, immigrants, or minorities.

Movies also made huge technological gains in the 1920s. At the beginning of the decade, movies were silent. Dialogue was written on the screen, and the only sound was a live organ or piano. The first film with a synchronized soundtrack was released in 1923, but it was the 1927 movie *The Jazz Singer* that made talkies widespread. Even though most of the movies made in the 1920s were in black and white and silent, the 1920s were one of the most prolific moviemaking eras in history, with an average of 800 movies made every year.

Like today, movies were more than just entertainment. They were another way to spread a common culture, especially as new technology began to introduce color, sound, and music. The clothing styles and the settings in movies gave viewers an example of what the good life was supposed to look like. The movies fed the consumer culture by showing people things they didn't even know they wanted—until they saw them on the big screen.

TALKIES

Talking pictures, or movies with sound, were called talkies in the 1920s. *The Jazz Singer* was a popular talkie that changed the way people thought about movies.

You can watch a scene from *The Jazz Singer*.

Through movies and newsreels, the average American suddenly had a window into other lifestyles and even foreign cultures. Once movies with sound became standard, they also became a way for musical trends to be shared around the country.

However, the rise and spread of popular culture in radio and movies only made the gap between traditionalists and modernists wider. Even as popular culture and the new, modern lifestyle reached the entire country, there were still many people who thought that their traditional values and beliefs were being attacked. And nowhere was this more evident than in one of the most famous trials in American history.

The rise in the status of movie stars showed people with a glamorous life that many aspired to.

1920s TIDBIT

An important medical discovery of 1928 was made completely by accident. A Scottish scientist named Dr. Alexander Fleming left some bacteria in a dish in his lab when he went away on vacation. When he returned, he found that mold had grown that had prevented any new germs from forming. Fleming's discovery would lead to the development of penicillin, the first antibiotic.

THE MONKEY TRIAL

The Scopes trial became a high-profile, public way for the modernists, who supported evolution, to go against the traditionalists, who believed in the traditional religious explanation for human origin.

You've learned that the 1920s was a time of struggle between traditional and modern values. Traditionalists were afraid that everything they valued was coming to an end, such as the old standards of behavior and thinking. Modernists no longer cared if society approved of their behavior. One result of this struggle was a wave of religious revivalism, especially in the American South.

In the summer of 1925, this struggle between traditionalists and modernists came to a very visible showdown in a Dayton, Tennessee, courtroom. A high school biology teacher named John Scopes was charged with teaching evolution in his classroom. Teaching evolution was illegal. Evolution, a theory made famous by the work of Charles Darwin, is the idea that man evolved from lower forms of life, such as apes, during millions of years. This goes against traditional religious teaching in the Bible, which says humans were created by God during the seven days it took God to create the entire universe.

Scopes was accused of breaking a Tennessee law that said it was unlawful "to teach any theory that denies the story of divine creation as taught by the Bible and to teach instead that man was descended from a lower order of animals." Going up against each other in court were two well-known lawyers. Clarence Darrow and the American Civil Liberties Union (ACLU) defended Scopes, while William Jennings Bryan argued against evolution and supported the fundamentalist Christian viewpoint. The trial ended up being more about the constitutionality of teaching or not teaching evolution, than about Scopes' crime.

VICTORY?

The anti-evolutionary groups claimed the trial as a victory. But Darrow and the ACLU succeeded in bringing the theory of evolution and the scientific evidence for it into the public's eye through the news coverage of the trial.

It was called the "trial of the century" and was attended by hundreds of reporters and spectators in the stifling heat of July. Bryan argued that the theory of evolution was simply "millions of guesses strung together," while Darrow questioned whether everything in the Bible should be taken as absolute truth. In the end, Scopes was found guilty and fined $100.

HITTING THE MOON?

Science in the 1920s was not limited to debating how humans came to be on Earth. Many other exciting and less controversial scientific discoveries took place at this time. One of them would lay the groundwork for space exploration.

In 1907, when Robert Goddard was a student at the Worcester Polytechnic Institute in Worcester, Massachusetts, he fired off a powder rocket in the basement of one of the school's buildings, creating a very visible cloud of smoke. Fortunately, he was not expelled for his experiment, because Goddard would later patent a rocket using liquid fuel and then a multi-stage rocket that used solid fuel.

Even today, teaching evolution in schools continues to be a hotly debated issue.

IN HIS OWN WORDS

"To me, personally, these tests, taken together, prove conclusively the practicality of the liquid-propelled rocket . . . " Goddard wrote this in a letter to Dr. C.G. Abbot of the Smithsonian Institute.

Read more of the letter and see a photograph of Goddard and his rocket frame.

Thanks to the many inventions of the Roaring Twenties, the modern age of airplane travel, communication, movies, cars, and space travel got its start. But these technological achievements aren't the only lasting legacy of the 1920s. The shift from the traditional to the modern would also include the arts and the lifestyles they both influenced and reflected.

Goddard not only realized the potential of rockets and space flight, he worked to make them practical as well. He would ultimately receive more than 70 patents for his work, and his contributions made modern space travel possible.

Goddard intrigued the 1920s public with the possibility of manned space flight, beginning with a January 1920 article about him in the *Boston Herald* newspaper. It was based on a scholarly paper that Goddard had released the previous day to the Smithsonian Institution, which was funding Goddard's research. The Smithsonian had put out a press release that said Goddard had invented a rocket that might make it possible to explore the outer regions of the air and perhaps even reach the moon.

The *Boston Herald* headline proclaimed, "New Rocket Devised By Prof. Goddard May Hit Face Of The Moon." Even though Goddard never specifically mentioned sending humans into space, it was suddenly a part of the popular culture. Music, cartoons, magazines, movies, and poetry soon included the manned rocket concept. Another scientific idea became part of the new, modern culture of America.

READING THE STATES

William Jennings Bryan was already famous before his involvement in the Scopes Trial. In 1896, 1900, and 1908, he was the Democratic candidate for the U.S. presidency.

- **For each of these elections, create a map that shows the states that Bryan won.** You can find these maps on the Internet at sites such as uselectionatlas.org. Can you find any similarities in the states that Bryan won in these three elections?

- **Use the information in these maps.** Can you predict how the people living in Dayton, Tennessee, would probably have responded to Bryan during the Scopes trial? Explain the reason behind your answer.

To investigate more, think about today's political divisions. Presidential election results often refer to red (Republican) and blue (Democratic) states. Find a map that shows the red and blue state results for a recent election. Can you draw any conclusions based on which states voted Republican or Democrat?

◄ **Inquire & Investigate**

VOCAB LAB

Write down what you think each word means: **assembly line, mass consumption, perishable, icon, newsreel, traditionalist,** and **modernist.**

Compare your definitions with those of your friends or classmates. Did you all come up with the same meanings? Turn to the text and glossary if you need help.

1920s TIDBIT

Americans were captivated by Charles Lindbergh and his daring flight.

Watch footage of Lindbergh and his plane here.

LOOK UP!

Two of the most famous skyscrapers in the world were constructed in New York City at the end of the Roaring Twenties. The Chrysler Building was started in 1928 and finished in 1931. With 77 floors, it is still the tallest brick building in the world, although it has a steel skeleton. The Empire State Building was the world's tallest building until the World Trade Center towers were built in 1970. Both the Chrysler Building and the Empire State Building have become cultural icons and symbols of New York City and the United States.

BUILT TO LAST

The 1920s saw a building boom in cities, and many of these new buildings were skyscrapers. It was only because of advancements in design, materials, and construction that these buildings were able to reach more than five or ten stories in height. As buildings grew taller, they had to be strong and able to withstand wind and weather.

Here's your chance to design and build a tower that can withstand the wind from a fan and support a tennis ball at least 18 inches off the ground.

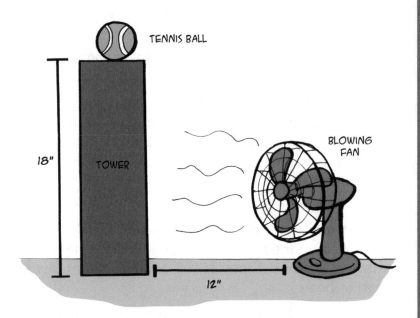

TENNIS BALL

18"

TOWER

BLOWING
FAN

12"

**Ideas for
Supplies** ▼

- building surface such
  as a tray, cardboard,
  or piece of wood
- electric fan
- printer paper or
  newspaper
- plastic drinking
  straws
- string
- masking or duct tape
- wooden skewers,
  chopsticks, or
  Popsicle sticks
- tennis ball

- **Using only these materials, design a tower that's
  at least 18 inches tall.** It must be strong enough to
  hold the tennis ball and resist the breeze from the
  fan. This activity can be done as a team in a classroom
  setting or at home by yourself. Once you decide on
  a design, go ahead and construct your tower.

- **Test your tower.** Place the fan 1 foot away from your
  tower. Turn the fan on low speed. Does the tower
  stay upright or tip over? Does the tennis ball remain
  on the top? If the tower can't stay upright and hold
  the tennis ball, then do some redesigning to fix the
  problem.

To investigate more, try setting the fan on high
speed. Does your tower need redesigning now? Try
designing a tower that can hold a heavier weight,
such as a softball or soccer ball. Can you construct
an even taller tower that is still stable? What other
building materials might you choose?

BUILD YOUR OWN ROCKET

Just as Robert Goddard created rocket technology in the 1920s, you can also build and fly your own rocket.

NOTE: The film canister must be the kind with a cap that fits inside the rim, not over the outside of the rim. Check with your local photography shop or drugstore to see if it has some to donate. You might also find one on the Internet.

- **Construct your rocket out of paper.** The diagram provided on the next page gives you some ideas on how to cut the shapes of the nose cone, fins, and rocket body.

- **Use trial and error.** What is the best way to wrap and tape the long strip to the film canister to create a tube of paper? Make sure that the lid end of the canister faces down so that it will be on the bottom of the tube. How many fins do you want to tape to the rocket tube? Can you design a nose cone section and tape it to the rocket's top? What purpose do you think the nose cone serves?

BLASTOFF!

On March 16, 1926, Robert Goddard successfully constructed and then launched the first rocket to use liquid fuel. This was as important an event as the Wright brothers launching their airplane in Kitty Hawk, North Carolina.

Watch Goddard's first liquid-fueled rocket take off.

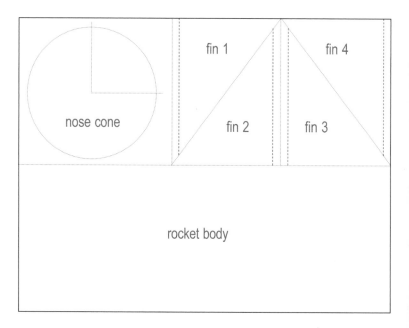

8½ x 11 paper

------- CUT -------
-------- FOLD --------

nose cone

fin 1

fin 4

fin 2

fin 3

rocket body

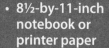
Ideas for Supplies ▼

- 8½-by-11-inch notebook or printer paper
- scissors
- plastic 35-mm film canister
- tape
- water
- effervescing (fizzing) antacid tablet, the kind taken for upset stomachs
- paper towels
- eye protection, such as safety glasses or goggles

- **Prepare your rocket to blast off!** Choose a place outside away from animals and people. Put on your safety goggles or glasses to protect your eyes. Turn the rocket upside down and remove the lid to the film canister. Carefully fill the canister about one-third full of water. Very quickly, drop one half of the antacid tablet into the canister, snap the lid on tightly, and stand your rocket on its launch platform, like a sidewalk or driveway. Stand back and watch your rocket to blast off!

To investigate more, consider what you can alter about your rocket's design to change the way it flies. How can you make it fly higher, faster, or in a different direction?

Chapter 4

Culture and All That Jazz

"THIS IS NOT A PIPE"

How did the music, art, and literature of the 1920s influence new culture and reflect changes in society?

THEY WENT TO THE BEST CLUBS.

Music, art, novels, and fashion not only showed that American culture was changing, but also spread that new culture all over the country and even the world.

What is culture? Strictly speaking, it's the arts and other means that show intellectual achievement. But popular culture goes a little further than that. It is the collective ideas and attitudes of a group at a certain time, including their tastes, activities, and the commercial products they use. Both of these types of culture were changing during the Roaring Twenties.

IT STARTS AT HOME

Many of the changes in popular culture and society in the 1920s came about through a new way of thinking about people—especially women—and the roles they played in society. Before this time, women were still expected to be at home. Their role was to keep house and raise children, always acting modestly and politely, with no real place in the outside world.

This traditional view was still tightly held by the traditionalists. But soon they were challenged by the New Woman of the era, a women who was symbolized by the flapper.

The flapper represented the new, modern woman. She smoked cigarettes, drank liquor in public, wore shorter skirts and silk stockings, and cut her hair short in a bob. She could wear makeup and dye her hair without being seen as a "bad" woman. Where well-dressed women once wore floor-length, heavy skirts, multiple petticoats, and corsets, flappers wore thin dresses with skirts that showed their knees.

The fashion fad of the 1920s was for women to look thin and almost boyish. This led to drastic diet and exercise regimes. Smoking cigarettes helped keep weight off, which was another point in their favor with flappers. Advertisers quickly saw opportunities for enticing women to buy cosmetics, diet aids, and other beauty supplies to help them achieve the look of the flapper.

Behavior also changed with the New Woman of the 1920s. Flappers were often restless, superficial, and only concerned about themselves. They no longer felt they had to live up to the traditional roles and values their mothers and grandmothers had contended with. They frequently went to nightclubs and speakeasies, where they danced, smoked, and drank illegal cocktails. The growing awareness of contraception also gave them more sexual freedom and a way to limit the number of children they had after they were married.

THE FUN OF BEING A FLAPPER

After spending so many generations at home caring for their families, many women were thrilled to get a taste of fun.

You can watch clips of flappers engaging with the world on their own terms.

BURNING OUT

One of Edna St. Vincent Millay's best-known poems sums up the poet's wish for adventure and an exciting life, just like many other modern women:

My Candle burns at both ends;

It will not last the night;

But ah, my foes, and oh, my friends—

It gives a lovely light.

A WOMAN'S PLACE . . .

Of course, most flappers eventually married and settled down, but even marriage and motherhood were easier than they had been. Inventions such as the washing machine, electric stove, refrigerator, and vacuum cleaner saved women a lot of time and energy when it came to housekeeping. Many new kinds of prepared and packaged foods made it easier to plan and provide meals for their families.

The 19th Amendment to the U.S. Constitution had given women the right to vote in 1920. Some women had already worked at jobs outside the home during World War I, when there was a shortage of men for those jobs. They found out what it was like to make their own money and enjoy more freedom.

There were more opportunities for women—especially single women—than ever before. Not only could they still have traditional women's jobs such as nursing, teaching, and working in a library, now they could also work in offices as secretaries, stenographers, typists, and file clerks. Women also worked in department stores as clerks, and sometimes moved up to merchandising, designing, and buying. Women could still work on their family farms or in textile mills.

Some women were successful in more creative careers, such as the arts. As writers, poets, actresses, and dancers, Dorothy Parker, Edna St. Vincent Millay, Clara Bow, and Martha Graham were all famous in the 1920s. They would contribute to an artistic culture that launched many artists and writers who are still read and recognized today.

THE LOST GENERATION

Some of the most famous writers of the 1920s were often referred to as the Lost Generation. They had come of age during World War I, and were disillusioned with the traditional morals and values they returned to. They no longer believed that if you acted in a virtuous and moral way, good things would happen to you.

The horrors of the war, where many young men died or were terribly wounded, made these writers feel that there was no point in following traditional behavior or morals. It made these young people aimless and unhappy and "lost." Ernest Hemingway, F. Scott Fitzgerald, and John Dos Passos were the three best-known writers of the Lost Generation, which also included Sherwood Anderson, Hart Crane, William Faulkner, Zelda Fitzgerald (who was also the epitome of the flapper), and Ford Madox Ford.

F. Scott Fitzgerald's novels, such as *The Great Gatsby*, showed characters living the modern life of the Jazz Age, going to parties and living wildly in order to hide a deeper unhappiness and loneliness. Hemingway also wrote about characters that had come out of the war feeling lost and disillusioned. Hemingway's writing style itself was new, with crisp, lean sentences that contrasted with the dense writing of the previous Victorian Age.

Many of these writers, as well as artists and composers, left the mainstream materialistic culture of the United States entirely and moved to places such as Paris. They produced some of the best-remembered works of the era while living a more bohemian lifestyle than they could have in America.

FLAPPERS AROUND THE WORLD

In the 1920s, women in the United States, Europe, and Australia were enjoying freedoms they'd never had before. But women who lived in the Middle East and many parts of Africa and Asia had to wait several more decades before they were free to pursue employment outside the home or even go to a dance club. Many women around the world are still waiting for social and political norms to change enough for them to work, vote, dance, drive, talk, and live as they choose.

The Lost Generation writers and artists experimented with new styles and themes to express their feelings toward postwar American society.

THE ART SCENE

PARIS—HOME AWAY FROM HOME

Many writers and artists left the United States to live cheaply in Paris in the 1920s.

Watch what life was like in 1920s Paris.

Writers were not the only ones making creative history during the 1920s. Artists, too, were experimenting with new mediums and new types of art that were drastically different from earlier eras. Several new styles were born, starting with dada. As with the Lost Generation writers, dadaist artists were disillusioned with modern American society after WWI. They left behind the traditions of realistic art that looked exactly like what it was representing, and developed a sort of nonsense art instead.

This nonsense art and related poetry were meant to express the meaninglessness of traditional values. Dada artists include Man Ray (a painter and photographer), Marcel Duchamp (who created art from found, everyday objects), and Beatrice Wood (an artist and potter).

The dada movement led to another artistic movement of the 1920s, surrealism. It started as a literary movement that was picked up by artists such as Max Ernst and Salvador Dalí. Surrealists created images consisting of what seemed like totally unrelated objects placed against mysterious backgrounds.

Surrealists were influenced by the work of Sigmund Freud, a famous psychoanalyst who believed that many of people's most important thoughts and feelings were buried in their subconscious minds. Surrealists attempted to access these hidden feelings through random or dreamlike images. Some of these artists, such as René Magritte, used realistic painting styles that made their paintings look almost like photographs. Other artists, such as Joan Miró and Paul Klee, used abstract shapes that did not resemble real objects at all.

ART DECO

One of the most beautiful and distinctive art movements was born during the 1920s. Called art deco, it is a modern art movement that started at the Exposition Internationale des Arts Décoratifs et Industriels Modernes, an art exhibit held in Paris in 1925. Art deco style uses simple, clean, geometric shapes that often look streamlined. It also combines traditional craft elements with Machine Age modern images and materials, which fit well with the modern feel of the 1920s. Materials include both manmade (plastic, Bakelite, glass, and concrete) and natural (jade, ivory, obsidian, chrome, and silver). Art Deco designs are used in decorative items, stained glass windows, textiles, and architecture.

There are art deco elements in many famous buildings, including the Chrysler Building and the Empire State Building in New York City.

Look at other examples of Art Deco design elements here.

A wave of new music, art, and literature by African Americans gained recognition from both black society and white society during the Harlem Renaissance.

See and hear what Harlem might have been like in the 1920s.

"I believe in Liberty for all men; the space to stretch their arms and their souls; the right to breathe and the right to vote, the freedom to choose their friends, enjoy the sunshine and ride on the railroads, uncursed by color."

—W.E.B. Du Bois published these words in 1920, a few decades before the civil rights movement started

IT HAPPENED IN HARLEM

In 1920s America, racial segregation could be seen in all aspects of American life. There were stores for whites, and separate stores for blacks. Whites rode at the front of the bus while blacks were only allowed in the back. "Whites only" signs were everywhere. There were even drinking fountains only for people with white skin. While this would not change until the civil rights movement began in the 1950s, the seeds of this change were planted in many places in the 1920s. Harlem was one of those places.

The Harlem neighborhood in New York City was originally planned as a neighborhood for white workers, for those who wanted to live outside the city and commute into the city to work. However, the neighborhood grew faster than the transportation network, and many white tenants moved out. Landlords began renting to African American tenants who had been pushed out of downtown housing or who had come from the South looking for better employment opportunities.

Between 1900 and 1920, the number of African Americans in Harlem doubled. The area, which was only 3 square miles (4.8 square kilometers) in size, had nearly 175,000 residents, making it the largest concentration of black people in the world at that time. African Americans brought their own businesses and institutions with them.

Harlem became a place where some of the newest and best African American artists, entrepreneurs, writers, and composers came together. It was also a center for politics and a new political push for civil rights.

Leaders included W.E.B. Du Bois, who helped found the National Association for the Advancement of Colored People (NAACP). Marcus Garvey started the Universal Negro Improvement Association and African Communities League (UNIA-ACL). These men encouraged African Americans to come together as communities and to be proud of their race and heritage.

These political, intellectual, and artistic movements came together in what would be called the Harlem Renaissance. Why was the Harlem Renaissance important? It empowered African Americans and served as a way for them to work for civil rights and equality through music and art and writing. It also pushed these arts into mainstream culture.

There were many black-owned magazines and newspapers, publishing the work of writers such as Langston Hughes and Zora Neale Hurston. Artists such as Palmer C. Hayden, Malvin Gray Johnson, and Laura Wheeler Waring created bold paintings as well as scenes of African American life. Augusta Savage sculpted in bronze, and prolific painter Aaron Douglas created illustrations and cover art for magazines and books. James Van Der Zee was known for his photographs.

Speakeasies also abounded in Harlem, including those such as the Cotton Club, which was decorated to look like a Southern plantation. Ironically, while all the performers were African American, only whites were allowed as customers. But it was an opportunity for whites to hear a type of music that was becoming more and more popular: jazz.

During the Harlem Renaissance, African Americans gained a new cultural identity and brought it to the wider world.

SLANG OF TOMORROW

The twenties was the first decade to emphasize youth culture over the older generations. Young people often use slang to create new words that become mainstream with time—some 1920s slang words are still used today!

dolled up: dressed up

bee's knees: an extraordinary person, thing, or idea; the ultimate

ritzy: elegant (from the hotel)

AND ALL THAT JAZZ

Jazz was not a completely new musical form in the 1920s, but because of its exuberant rhythms and sounds it became associated with the wild and carefree living of the era. In fact, the 1920s would come to be called the Jazz Age. The music spread through the radio and the popularity of records and sheet music.

But what exactly is jazz? It's a lively form of music that has several key characteristics: swing, syncopation, improvisation, bent notes, and distinctive voices. Swing is the rhythmic movement that makes the music exciting and makes listeners want to sway, dance, or snap their fingers. Syncopation makes the rhythm unexpected because it places the accents or emphasized beats in unusual places that the listener's ear doesn't expect. Improvisation is also an important element and means that jazz musicians do not strictly play the music as it was written. Instead, they might change the rhythm, the melody, or the harmony. Jazz musicians almost never play a song exactly the same way twice.

JELLY ROLL BLUES

Musician Jelly Roll Morton claimed that he invented jazz in 1922. That's probably an exaggeration, since no one person could really have invented this musical form, but he did compose some of the first real jazz music. His "Jelly Roll Blues" is considered to be the first serious piece of jazz music ever published.

Listen to a version recorded in 1926.

Jazz originally drew on ragtime, gospel, black spiritual songs, West African rhythms, and European harmonies.

The use of bent notes means that jazz players often use notes that can't be played on a piano. With an instrument such as a guitar, saxophone, trombone, or the human voice, they could slide between one note and the next, bending the traditional notes of a scale into notes that are found in the spaces between those standard notes. This gives jazz music a feeling of mystery, tension, and energy.

Different jazz musicians play with their own particular tone, rhythms, and improvisational style. These different voices were what made many of the musicians of the Jazz Age into stars. These included Louis Armstrong, Duke Ellington, and Cab Calloway, plus big bands such as Paul Whiteman's orchestra and Bix Beiderbecke's dance band and jazz blues singers Bessie Smith and Lena Horne. Billie Holiday began singing in Harlem jazz clubs as a teenager.

Jazz also brought with it a craze for dancing, and not the dignified traditional waltzes of the older generations. Young people danced the Charleston and the Black Bottom, usually to big dance orchestras with as many as 12 musicians. Again, the wild and energetic forms of dance became linked with the wilder, modern generation, emphasizing the identity of the 1920s as the Jazz Age. Jazz quickly moved out of the Harlem speakeasies and nightclubs and into the new, popular, modern culture.

1920s TIDBIT

The Harlem Renaissance wasn't limited to jazz music. Singer Marian Anderson, who would be the first black woman to sing with the Metropolitan Opera, started singing in church choirs at the age of 6. By the time she was a teen, she was competing in singing contests in New York City.

MORE SLANG

baloney: nonsense

swanky: fashionable and expensive

cat's meow: something splendid or stylish

you slay me: that's funny

LITERARY VOICES

Ernest Hemingway and F. Scott Fitzgerald were two of the best-known writers of the 1920s. However, they had very different and distinct literary styles.

> "Money cannot buy health, but I'd settle for a diamond-studded wheelchair."
>
> —Dorothy Parker, writer and poet

• **Read the excerpts from Hemingway and Fitzgerald.** Compare and contrast their styles. What differences can you find in their writing? Are there any similarities? Which excerpt seems to convey the feeling of the 1920s better? Which style do you prefer?

Ernest Hemingway, *The Sun Also Rises*

"I know a girl in Strasbourg who can show us the town," I said.

Somebody kicked me under the table. I thought it was accidental and went on: "She's been there two years and knows everything there is to know about the town. She's a swell girl."

I was kicked again under the table and, looking, saw Frances, Robert's lady, her chin lifting and her face hardening.

"Hell," I said, "why go to Strasbourg? We could go up to Bruges, or to the Ardennes."

Cohn looked relieved. I was not kicked again. I said good-night and went out. Cohn said he wanted to buy a paper and would walk to the corner with me. "For God's sake," he said, "why did you say that about that girl in Strasbourg for? Didn't you see Frances?"

"No, why should I? If I know an American girl that lives in Strasbourg what the hell is it to Frances?"

"It doesn't make any difference. Any girl. I couldn't go, that would be all."

"Don't be silly."

"You don't know Frances. Any girl at all. Didn't you see the way she looked?"

HOW DOES HEMINGWAY CONSTRUCT SUCH SIMPLE BUT VIVID IMAGERY?

F. Scott Fitzgerald, *The Great Gatsby*

I looked back at my cousin, who began to ask me questions in her low, thrilling voice. It was the kind of voice that the ear follows up and down, as if each speech is an arrangement of notes that will never be played again. Her face was sad and lovely with bright things in it, bright eyes and a bright passionate mouth, but there was an excitement in her voice that men who had cared for her found difficult to forget: a singing compulsion, a whispered "Listen," a promise that she had done gay, exciting things just a while since and that there were gay, exciting things hovering in the next hour.

I told her how I had stopped off in Chicago for a day on my way East, and how a dozen people had sent their love through me.

"Do they miss me?" she cried ecstatically.

"The whole town is desolate. All the cars have the left rear wheel painted black as a mourning wreath, and there's a persistent wail all night along the north shore."

"How gorgeous! Let's go back, Tom. To-morrow!" Then she added irrelevantly: "You ought to see the baby."

"I'd like to."

"She's asleep. She's three years old. Haven't you ever seen her?"

"Never."

"Well, you ought to see her. She's — —!"

> To investigate more, write your own one-paragraph character description, based on either Hemingway's or Fitzgerald's style. Which comes easiest for you? Why do you think both styles were attractive to readers during the 1920s? Can you think of contemporary writers who write like either of these authors?

VOCAB LAB

Write down what you think each word means: **intellectual**, **flapper**, **disillusioned**, **materialistic**, **bohemian**, **surrealism**, **Harlem Renaissance**, and **syncopation**.

Compare your definitions with those of your friends or classmates. Did you all come up with the same meanings? Turn to the text and glossary if you need help.

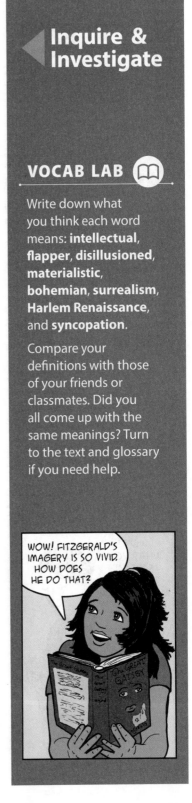

LET'S EAT

Many packaged, frozen, and convenience foods made their first appearances in the 1920s. Where women once made their families' meals from scratch, now they could use premade foods and ingredients to create meals. Some familiar brand names that made their debuts during this time included Wonder Bread, Welch's grape jelly, Kool-Aid, Hostess Cakes, Rice Krispies, and things such as frozen vegetables, instant coffee, and canned goods.

Prepared foods and household appliances made housework less of a chore. It freed up more time for women to pursue their own interests, often outside the house.

- **Research what convenience foods were available during the 1920s.** Then create a menu for a basic family dinner, using as many of these new convenience foods as possible. How long might it have taken the average cook to create this meal using these "shortcut" food items?

- **Now research recipes in an average cookbook, such as *Betty Crocker* or *Joy of Cooking*.** Estimate how long it would take to make the same dinner from scratch, with no convenience foods. Can you estimate how much longer cooking from scratch might have taken?

- **Finally, see if you can create the same dinner menu using modern convenience foods, such as microwave entrees, etc.** Create a chart that shows your three dinners and the time it takes to cook each one. Analyze and compare the cost of premade food versus the cost of ingredients.

To investigate more, consider the current slow food trend, which encourages people to cook with local, organic ingredients. Why might this be better? Can you compare cooking with standard convenience foods, in terms of time and money, to cooking using slow-food ingredients?

WOW! WHAT YOU SAVE IN TIME YOU MAKE UP FOR IN ADDITIVES AND CHEMICALS! YUM!

AN ARTIST'S EYE

The 1920s saw the rise of many artists we know well today. Each had his or her own distinctive style. New art movements such as surrealism and dada moved American art from realism to more abstract and modern styles. Become a student of art history and learn from the great artists of the 1920s.

- **Study the following paintings:**
  - » René Magritte, *The False Mirror*
  - » Aaron Douglas, *Aspiration*
  - » Georgia O'Keeffe, *Blue and Green Music*
  - » Salvador Dalí, *The Persistence of Memory*

- **Does one particular artist's style appeal to you more than the others'?** Note their use of color. Are their images stylized or realistic? What sort of message you think each painting is conveying?

- **Create your own piece of art in the style of one of these artists.** You can use any medium you want. Be sure to give your artwork a title!

"If the dream is a translation of waking life, waking life is also a translation of the dream."

—René Magritte, surrealist painter

To investigate more, try creating another piece of art in a different artist's style. How do you change your own style to show the difference in artists?

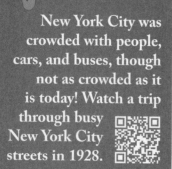

New York City was crowded with people, cars, and buses, though not as crowded as it is today! Watch a trip through busy New York City streets in 1928.

ADVERTISING ON THE ROAD

In 1925, the Burma-Vita company found a new way to advertise its Burma-Shave shaving cream. The company created a series of six small signs that were posted a short distance apart along a road. Motorists read the signs in order as they drove past. The small red-and-white signs were often funny, with a punch line at the end.

THE BEARDED LADY
TRIED A JAR
SHE'S NOW
A FAMOUS
MOVIE STAR
BURMA-SHAVE

IF YOU THINK
SHE LIKES
YOUR BRISTLES
WALK BARE-FOOTED
THROUGH SOME THISTLES
BURMA-SHAVE

IF YOU DON'T KNOW
WHOSE SIGNS THESE ARE
YOU CAN'T HAVE
DRIVEN VERY FAR
BURMA-SHAVE

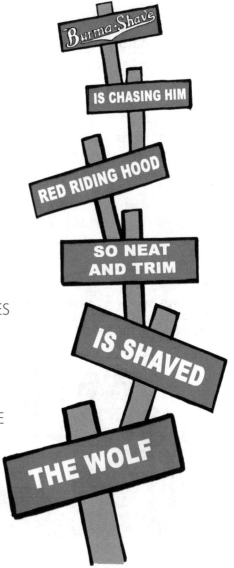

- **Now it's your turn to create your own set of signs.** What do you want to advertise? Can you write your own Burma-Shave ad or do you want to promote another product that was available during the 1920s? Start by writing the verses so that they can be separated into five or six separate signs. Which sign usually had the punch line for the verse?

- **Using strips of posterboard, create five or six strips, one for each sign.** If you want, you can even cut signs out of wood and attach them to stakes so that they can be stuck into the ground. Burma-Shave signs were traditionally red with white lettering, but if you're advertising another product you might want to choose different colors.

- **Carefully paint each sign with part of the verse, ending with the name of the product you're advertising.** If you've made your signs out of poster board, hang them on the wall so that they read sequentially from top to bottom. If you've made them out of wood, you can stick them in the ground in order, with each sign about two to three feet apart.

  » **NOTE:** Because you're pretending to advertise a product, don't post your signs beside a road. However, you might want to use this same method to advertise your school's next car wash or other fundraiser!

To investigate more, consider whether Burma-Shave signs were more effective than standard billboards with an entire advertisement in one place. Why or why not?

Inquire & Investigate

MORE SLANG

It isn't surprising that many new slang words of the 1920s described cars. These included boiler, bucket, bus (a big car), crate, flivver (a Ford), iron, hogs (a gas-guzzling car), and jalopy (an old car).

1920s TIDBIT

You can watch flappers dancing the charleston, popular dance in the 1920s.

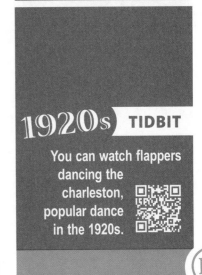

Chapter 5
Not Invited to the Party

Did everyone share
in the prosperity
of the 1920s?

The 1920s were only roaring for those people who enjoyed greater prosperity. There were many others who lived in poverty and did not share the rest of the country's good times.

It's easy to think of the Roaring Twenties as being a time when everyone had money and was focused on living the good life and having fun. Does it sound like the era was one big party? There were many people who weren't invited to that party. Living below the poverty line means not earning enough money to buy the very basics of food, clothing, and housing. By 1928, the number of people who lived below the poverty line was an estimated 42 percent of the population.

DOWN ON THE FARM

Farmers did not share in the good life of the 1920s. And since farming also affected people who made their living from farm-related services and equipment, a total of about 30 million people in the United States relied on farming for their living.

In some ways, American farming was more efficient than ever before, with new machines such as combines and harvesters making it easier to grow more crops. The result of this, however, was that farmers grew more food than Americans could eat. During WWI, it was easy to sell the surplus food to Europe. But once European farmers recovered from the war and were able to produce enough food themselves, this market dried up.

The U.S. government also implemented tariffs that made it expensive for foreign goods to be sold in the United States. A tariff is a kind of tax. If other countries could not easily sell their goods to America, then they had less money to spend on American goods. In response to American tariffs, Europe put tariffs on U.S. products destined for European markets, making U.S. crops even more expensive in Europe.

At the same time, Canadian farmers were growing so much grain that they were competing with American farmers on the world market. Barley, a grain used to make beer, was no longer in great demand because of Prohibition. As a result, there was too much grain and not enough buyers. Because of this overproduction, the price of grain fell, which ruined many smaller farms. In the 1920s, more than 3 million farm families were making less than $1,000 a year. This is the equivalent of a family earning about $13,500 in 2012.

Some farmers managed to do well. Very large farms in the midwest that grew huge amounts of grain and corn, as well as the big fruit growers in California and Florida, could grow and ship their crops in large quantities. But for small farmers and the laborers who worked for them, times kept getting worse.

To keep going, farmers borrowed money by taking on mortgages. When they couldn't pay their mortgages, they were either evicted or forced to sell their properties. As a result, from 1920 to 1950, the number of farms in the United States declined for the first time in history. For farm laborers, new equipment often meant that their labor was no longer needed, and they either became migrant workers in places such as California or moved to the larger cities to find work.

AN UNEQUAL DIVISION

One of the economic problems of the 1920s was inequality. The top 5 percent of the U.S. population earned 33 percent of the country's income. At the same time, 60 percent of Americans earned less than $2,000 a year. Most of the Americans living below the poverty line were farmers, African Americans, and immigrants.

Many farmers had no choice but to see their farms sold off by the bank when they couldn't pay their mortgages. However, their neighbors often came to their rescue. During bank foreclosure auctions, neighbors often showed up and placed a tiny bid—maybe 5 cents—on an item, such as a piece of farm machinery. Then the rest of the neighbors crowded around the auctioneer to keep anyone else from bidding. As a result, the auctioneer had to sell the item for 5 cents. Sometimes an entire farm auction resulted in only $5 or $6, which legally the bank had to accept as full payment on the farmer's debt.

Other times, the farmer himself would place a low bid on his items, and the rest of the auction attendees would refuse to bid. In this way, a farmer could get his entire collection of equipment back for a very low price.

Children were expected to work on the farm with their parents. According to the 1920 Census Bureau, more than 600,000 children worked on family farms, which was half of the total number of kids involved in child labor. But farm kids weren't so different from their town and city classmates. They liked the same entertainment that urban kids did, such as listening to the radio and going to the movies. Because they lived in rural areas, they might not have electricity, which limited how many modern appliances they had, including radios, refrigerators, and washing machines. This often made farm kids feel discontented. Older kids often left farms to look for jobs in the city, where modern life was much more exciting in comparison.

One of the best-known songs of the early twenties was called "How Ya Gonna Keep 'Em Down on the Farm." Even though the song was aimed at young men who had been overseas during WWI, it was still applicable to farm teens a few years later:

> How ya gonna keep 'em down on the farm
>
> After they've seen Paree'
>
> How ya gonna keep 'em away from Broadway
>
> Jazzin around and paintin' the town
>
> How ya gonna keep 'em away from harm, that's a mystery
>
> They'll never want to see a rake or plow
>
> And who the deuce can parleyvous a cow?
>
> How ya gonna keep 'em down on the farm
>
> After they've seen Paree'

1920s **TIDBIT**

Why didn't most farmers share in the prosperity of the 1920s? Consider the price of a bushel of wheat. In 1920, a farmer could get $183 for a bushel of wheat. By 1924, the price had fallen to just 38 cents a bushel.

Sharecroppers often ended up moving from one area to another at the end of the harvest, seeking a better place. Many landlords encouraged this because it kept tenants from becoming established and working their way up to better tenancy levels.

Farming conditions were the worst in the South, especially for those who were part of a system known as sharecropping. Sharecroppers usually rented their land from the landlord who owned it. The sharecropper gave a percentage of his or her crop to the landlord in payment for the land use. This system began after the Civil War and the end of slavery as a way to keep former slaves working the land in the South.

After 1900, the number of white farmers in the sharecropping system increased. The farming difficulties of the 1920s led to almost half of all white farmers and 77 percent of black farmers no longer owning their own land. They just worked within the sharecropping system for other landowners.

There were different levels of sharecropping. At the bottom of the heap were the pure sharecroppers who rarely came out ahead at harvest time, often owing their landlords more for their "furnish" than they would receive from the crop sales. Furnish was the name for the items they'd been given, such as shelter and tools. This meant they were forced to remain on the land because they owed money to the landlords. Year after year, many sharecroppers went deeper and deeper into debt.

If a sharecropper was able to accumulate some of his own equipment and save some money, he could become a share tenant. At this level, a share tenant kept as much as two-thirds or three-quarters of the crop instead of just half. The more they could provide of their own furnish, the greater the profits from the crops.

Some share tenants were able to arrive at the point where all that was required from the landlord was the use of the land. These people could then become cash tenants who simply paid fixed rental fees for the land. Cash tenants kept all of the proceeds from their crops.

Unfortunately, during the 1920s, most sharecropping farmers were moving down in the system instead of up. In the South, the system revolved around cotton, and cotton prices were falling. Crop failures, low prices for cotton, ill health, soil that was worn out from too much farming, and poor management often resulted in farmers either losing their own farms and becoming sharecroppers or moving from cash or share tenants down to just sharecroppers. Nature also played a part in the form of drought, insects, and extreme weather that could damage or even destroy a crop.

"There was a man had been, was working sharecrop for a gentleman and naturally, he couldn't read or either write. And every year, regardless of how much cotton he made he would just bring him out so he would have just a little bit left."

—Hughset Childes, sharecropper

1920s TIDBIT

Sharecropping was a system that affected black farmers more than white farmers. By the 1920s, nearly three-quarters of all black farmers, and a third of white farmers, were sharecroppers. However, nearly all of the landowners were white. For many black farmers, sharecropping was little better than slavery.

The government did attempt to help farmers during the 1920s. Because of the recession in farming, two lawmakers—Senator Charles McNary of Oregon and U.S. Representative Gilbert Haugen from Iowa—sponsored bills that were designed to bring farmers' standard of living up to the same level as industrial workers. Their intent was to help farmers receive more money for their crops. The idea was for the federal government to buy surplus harvests of cotton, corn, rice, hogs, tobacco, and wheat and then sell them in foreign markets, boosting agricultural prices for U.S. farmers.

The first McNary-Haugen Agricultural Surplus Control Bill made its way through Congress in 1924 and was passed in 1927, only to be vetoed by President Calvin Coolidge a few days later. A second bill was passed by Congress in 1928, but this one was also vetoed by Coolidge. He objected to supporting farmers with a bill like this, feeling that it would only contribute to the problem of agricultural overproduction. It wasn't until 1929 that a compromise bill, the Agricultural Marketing Act, was signed by the new president, Herbert Hoover.

The Agricultural Credits Act of 1923 had also been meant to provide relief for farmers. This act was designed to give farmers credit and loans specifically for them. A network of 12 Federal Intermediate Credit Banks established in different parts of the country were authorized to loan money to farm cooperative associations. These associations could then turn around and lend it to farmers. While this helped some farmers, it did not help with the basic problem: overproduction.

Farmers themselves were split in their support of the McNary-Haugen bills. Some critics felt that real farmers favored the bill, while wealthy "gentlemen" farmers, or farmers who were actually merchants and businessmen, really didn't need the bill as much and didn't bother to fight for it. The bills created a great deal of debate from all farmers on both sides of the issue.

NEW CITIES, OLD INDUSTRIES

The cycle of sharecropping often left families without enough money for the basics of life and drew them deeper into debt every year. Sharecropping also spurred the movement of African Americans northward to find work in cities. However, most of the jobs they found in the North were the lowest-paid positions, usually menial jobs. Many of the women worked as low-paid domestic servants in wealthy white households. While blacks may have found a new sense of community in the Harlem neighborhood of New York City, it was so crowded that people often took turns sleeping in beds. One person slept while the other went to work.

African Americans were not the only workers to suffer from low wages. Many factory workers, even in the age of prosperity and new inventions, worked in low-wage jobs in what were called old industries—coal, textiles, and raw materials. These industries were either being replaced by newer industries, being modernized to the point where fewer workers were needed, or suffered from overproduction.

How does the poverty rate of 42 percent in 1928 compare to the poverty rate now? In 2012, about 15 percent of the U.S. population lived below the poverty line. But what hasn't changed is that the top 5 percent of the population earns more than one-third of the country's income.

1920s TIDBIT

One of the ways that jazz music flourished was because of "rent parties." A person who rented a house or apartment threw a party with music, then asked for donations from the partygoers to help pay the rent.

UNION ACTION

A union is an organization of workers that is formed to protect the rights and interests of the union members. When workers are organized, they can fight together for higher wages and better working conditions. They can go on strike if the employer won't give them what they feel is right. But strikes don't always work.

Workers in the coal industry suffered because oil and gas were beginning to replace coal as primary energy sources. More coal was being mined than could be sold in the market, which led to falling wages for miners and mine closures. By 1929, the average coal miner was making only a third of the national average for income. In addition to closed mines and dropping wages, safety standards were also relaxed and working days were lengthened.

Miners who belonged to unions even went on a four-month strike in 1922, with 600,000 miners trying to force their companies to improve conditions. But the strike did not work. Non-union miners simply charged less for coal and grabbed more of the market. Earlier mining strikes in West Virginia were ended by state troopers, who used force.

Textile workers were losing their jobs as well. As fashions changed to the new, modern flapper style, clothing required less cloth than when women wore dresses with yards and yards of heavy, long skirts. Less cloth meant fewer workers manufacturing it. In Tennessee in 1927, a group of textile workers who were receiving only 18 cents an hour for a 56-hour week went on strike. Force was used to end that strike as well.

THEY STARTED AS BOYS...

...AND ENDED UP AS MEN.

AS INDIVIDUALS... THEY WERE VOICELESS.

UNIONS

The 1920s were a critical time for the labor movement and unions. During World War I, unions were valued partners in winning the war. But afterward, unions were seen as putting their needs ahead of the welfare of the country. Employers refused to raise wages, and as a result, hundreds of strikes took place around 1919. The public complained about the inconveniences caused by strikes. Employers actively campaigned against unions, even claiming that they were communist organizations. Unions argued that they were working for democracy and freedom for their members.

Because of the country's overall prosperity, labor unions were not very successful during the twenties. Generally during this time, when workers had a dispute with their employers, the federal government sided with the employers. The U.S. Supreme Court even declared two state laws unconstitutional: one that banned child labor and one that set a minimum wage for female workers.

The number of workers belonging to unions shrank, from 5.1 million workers in 1920 to only 3.6 million in 1929. More workers who needed to keep their jobs did not have unions to protect their interests. It wasn't until the Great Depression of the 1930s that the unions became powerful enough to improve the plight of workers.

COMING TO AMERICA

In addition to farmers, African Americans, and factory workers, another group of people in the United States suffered from poverty during this time. The number of immigrants allowed to come to America was limited, but those who did arrive often faced discrimination that made finding work and a place to live very difficult. Because immigrants were often less educated than native-born Americans and may not have spoken English, they took whatever work they could find. Many were employed in factories, but they usually had the worst jobs and the lowest pay. Because immigrants were desperate for work, and weren't likely to complain or strike, some employers welcomed them to their factories.

A large number of immigrants worked in the construction industry, because there was a building boom in the 1920s. Since immigrants were a cheap source of labor, they drove down the overall wages for all workers in the industry. Throughout the 1920s, the wages of construction workers rose only 4 percent. This was partly because of cheap immigrant labor and partly because the industry was using more machines and workers were no longer needed for certain jobs. Overall, the unemployment rate of immigrants remained high throughout the decade.

While these groups of farmers, African Americans, and immigrants did not share the exuberance and party atmosphere of the 1920s, they would not be alone for long. There were warning signs that things were not as rosy as they seemed, and soon the party would be over for everyone.

"It had been represented that many would-be immigrants arriving at the port of New York had been refused admission and been sent home again, because they had happened to arrive a few hours after their country's legal quota for the month, under the new law, had been filled; and thus after parents had been admitted to the United States their children were sent back, or children were admitted and their parents sent back."

—*The Independent,* Spring/Summer 1921

COME NORTH!

Many African Americans traveled north during the 1920s to find better work opportunities. Some came because companies in the north were actively seeking workers for typically lower-paying jobs. If you owned a company that needed workers during this time, how might you persuade people to come north to work for you?

- **Research some of the companies that were hoping to attract these workers.** What jobs were available and what wages might they pay? Were there any other incentives that could convince people to move hundreds of miles from home? How can you use this information to create a poster that makes moving north to work for you an appealing option for a poor sharecropper in the South.

- **What materials would have been available at the time to design and create a poster?** You could have used paint, but computer graphics and copy machines were not invented yet. What else was available?

- **What words and images could you use to entice African American workers to move north?** What overall tone will your poster have?

To investigate more, imagine you are a worker in a big city who fears your job will be taken by someone coming from the South. What kind of poster would you create to protest this migration and convince other workers like you to complain?

Inquire & Investigate

VOCAB LAB

Write down what you think each word means: **poverty**, **tariff**, **sharecropper**, **debt**, **recession**, **menial**, **union**, and **strike**.

Compare your definitions with those of your friends or classmates. Did you all come up with the same meanings? Turn to the text and glossary if you need help.

GOOD TIMES, BAD TIMES

Depending on your perspective, the Roaring Twenties were either a time of prosperity and fun or filled with economic hardship. Here's your chance to examine both sides of the story.

- **Choose two perspectives from the 1920s to role play.** How would a flapper, living in the city and enjoying all the benefits of being a modern woman, view the world? How might a farm wife living in the Midwest, whose family is suffering from the poor farm economy, see things differently?

- **With a friend, choose who debates each side, and prepare arguments about whether the overall U.S. economy is good or bad.** Even though each role has its own perceptions about what life is like, could each also have a sense of the larger economy? How might the farm wife respond to arguments about the rising stock market or the affordability of modern household conveniences? How would the flapper respond to information about falling crop prices?

- **Now consider a debate between a prosperous 1920s businessman in the city, and a poor sharecropper in the South.** How would their viewpoints differ from each other, and why?

To investigate more, hold the same debate about today's economy. Is our economy improving? Are there more jobs or fewer? Are living conditions good for everyone or just a few groups? How might two different people see things from different perspectives?

ARRIVING IN A NEW LAND

Inquire & Investigate

While immigration was severely curtailed in the 1920s, there were still many people who arrived in America from foreign countries. They came hoping to start a new life. Using a blank, unlined notebook, make a scrapbook for an immigrant arriving at Ellis Island, New York.

- **What might be included in an immigrant's scrapbook?** Here are some ideas to get you started.
    - » a steamship ticket from steerage class
    - » family passports
    - » maps of New York
    - » photos of family members or the home the immigrant left behind
    - » letters from someone already in New York, telling the immigrant about life there
    - » postcards of New York
    - » journal entries describing the experience of being processed at Ellis Island
    - » descriptions of the immigrant's new home
    - » anything else you can think of, which might have been saved by an immigrant to document the experience of coming to America
- **Think about how to obtain these items and images.** Can you find them online? Will you create them yourself? What are some other sources you can turn to for a variety of items for your scrapbook?

> To investigate more, imagine that you are a modern immigrant coming to America from another part of the world. What items might you include in your scrapbook?

YOU CAN'T COME HERE

Immigrants arriving in New York between 1892 and 1954 passed through Ellis Island. Amazingly, one-third of the American population has an ancestor who came to America via Ellis Island.

The Immigration Act of 1924 severely limited the number of immigrants allowed to come into the United States each year, based on their countries of origin.

Take a look at how many people from each country were allowed into the United States during 1924 to 1925.

Chapter 6 ▶
The Party's Over

What brought the
Roaring Twenties
to an end?

The Roaring Twenties ended with the Stock Market Crash of 1929, but there were signs all along that the good times could not last.

Nothing lasts forever, and the wild excitement, optimism, and wealth of the Roaring Twenties was no exception. This decade of amazing inventions, new freedoms, and a modern way of life was followed by a decade that was almost completely the opposite. And while it's easy to say that the 1920s era came to an abrupt halt with the Stock Market Crash of 1929, there were warning signs throughout the decade of what was coming. It was one of the biggest after-party letdowns in history: the Great Depression.

"ABSOLUTELY SOUND"

During the 1920s, it was a national craze to purchase stocks on the stock market. It seemed as though there was no end to the possibility of becoming rich, simply by buying and selling stocks.

Before President Calvin Coolidge left office in March 1929, he is thought to have said that the stock market was "absolutely sound." There was no reason not to believe him. In July 1929, the craze for buying stocks—whether or not the purchaser actually had the money—was at its peak.

People didn't seem to care if the company whose stocks they were buying was a good investment or not. They simply wanted to be part of the rush to buy as much stock as they possibly could. This was a period of wild, uncontrolled speculation, and stock prices were pushed to a level that was completely unrealistic.

For nearly a century, critics have blamed Coolidge for contributing to the stock market craze by saying that the stock market was absolutely sound as he ended his presidency. But new research indicates he may have never uttered the words "absolutely sound" in reference to the stock market. Does it matter either way?

While this frenzy of stock buying was under way, there were plenty of signs that the U.S. economy was not in very good shape. Production at many factories had already declined, and unemployment had risen as a result. Some of this was due to the uneven distribution of wealth in the country. Since a small percentage of the American people had most of the money, most Americans had far less purchasing power and bought fewer goods. Stocks for manufacturing companies, however, were still valued much higher than they were really worth. In addition, wages were low and people had more debt than ever due to easy consumer credit and buying stocks on margin. Banks were holding many large loans that they could not call in for payment.

MORE SLANG

the real McCoy: the real thing

spiffy: an elegant appearance

putting on the Ritz: doing something in high style

java or joe: coffee

1920s TIDBIT

Studs Terkel, the well-known American author of the book *Hard Times: An Oral History of the Great Depression*, recalled the atmosphere in 1929.

"In 1929 it was strictly a gambling casino with loaded dice. I saw shoeshine boys buying $50,000 worth of stock with a $500 down payment. A cigar [company] stock at the time was selling for $114 a share. The market collapsed. The $114 stock dropped to $2, and the company president jumped out of the window of his Wall Street office."

The phrase "Dead Cat Bounce" comes from the saying, "Even a dead cat will bounce if it falls from a great height." This means that even stocks that are losing their value might rally for a moment, simply because they had been so overvalued to start.

DEAD CAT BOUNCE

The stock market peaked on September 3, 1929, with a record high number of stock transactions. But shortly after, a decline set in, carrying through into early October. On October 18, stock prices really began to fall, and shareholders began to panic. On October 24, nicknamed Black Thursday, a record number of 12,894,650 shares were traded as people tried to sell off their stocks.

Investment companies and leading banks attempted to quell the panic by buying up large blocks of stock, which rallied the market a bit the next day. This is known as a "dead cat bounce," a term used on Wall Street to represent a small, brief recovery in the prices of falling stocks. But the fall continued into the next week, and on October 29, 1929, nicknamed Black Tuesday, the market plummeted as 16,410,030 shares were traded.

Investors lost millions of dollars and most were completely wiped out. Stocks were now worth only about 20 percent of their value at the market's peak. People who had purchased stock on margin, at those peak prices, now suddenly had to pay back what they'd borrowed with money that they didn't have. Investors reacted with despair and desperation.

Banks had invested heavily in the stock market as well as real estate. When the market crashed, they lost the money that belonged to their investors. People began to panic as word spread that the banks had lost too much money. Millions lined up outside their banks to withdraw cash, which simply wasn't there.

The Great Depression arrived quickly as businesses shut down and people lost their jobs. Unemployment rose to 25 percent. For most people, their debts and mortgages stayed the same, but they no longer had any money to pay for them. As more and more people lost their jobs, they had no money for the most basic necessities, even food. Some people were forced into extreme living situations. One couple evicted from their New York City apartment lived in a cave in Central Park for a year.

Banks were saddled with properties that they had to foreclose upon and yet were now worth very little. Many banks—more than 9,000 between 1930 and 1932—simply shut their doors.

THE GREAT DEPRESSION

By 1932, one of every four American workers was unemployed. But unlike previous economic downturns, which usually only affected the poorest workers, this depression affected many more people than ever before, rich and poor alike. There were also more people living in cities than ever before: more than half of the nation. These people could not feed themselves from food grown on their farms, as they once might have. Without jobs or income, they could not afford a place to live, food to eat, or anything else.

Farmers were still struggling, as they had throughout the 1920s. But the situation was about to get even worse. The land was beginning to show the effects of generations of abuse. Fertile land had been exhausted, trees cut down, and prairie sod cut up and plowed under in order to grow wheat. Without grassy roots to hold the soil in place, droughts and high winds dried out the soil and blew it away.

"Ten men in our country could buy the whole world and ten million can't buy enough to eat."

—Will Rogers

AFTER THEIR LIVES WERE RUINED THERE WAS NOWHERE LEFT TO GO...

...BUT WEST.

STUDENT LOANS

Today, there's a new kind of debt for Americans to worry about. In 2012, Americans owed more than $900 billion in student loan debt. This is money borrowed to help pay for college and graduate school.

Oklahoma, the Texas Panhandle, New Mexico, Kansas, and Colorado experienced "black" blizzards, which were dust storms so severe they darkened the skies. The dust choked cattle and buried buildings in drifts of dirt. This time and place became known as the Dust Bowl, and because of it, many farmers, who were already suffering as a result of the 1920s and the Depression, became homeless. They began moving across the country, seeking employment.

Other American families that could no longer pay their mortgages lost their homes. If they were fortunate, they could move in with relatives. If they had no one to turn to, they might end up living in Hoovervilles, which were small camps of shacks made out of scrap wood, cardboard, and anything else that might keep the weather out. These camps were named after President Herbert Hoover, who was blamed by many for not doing more to help people in need. By 1933, a million Americans were living in Hoovervilles.

A NEW DEAL

The Great Depression lasted through the 1930s until World War II, when increased production helped bring back industry. President Franklin Roosevelt was elected in 1932. His New Deal programs also helped get the country back on its feet with many programs intended to get Americans back to work. New Deal programs regulated the stock market and insured bank deposits to guarantee that people who put their money in banks would not lose it as they had in 1929. Labor unions were encouraged, child labor was virtually eliminated, work hours were limited, and electricity was brought to people who lived in rural areas.

Some New Deal programs are still in place today, such as the Securities and Exchange Commission (SEC) to regulate the stock market and the Federal Deposit Insurance Corporation (FDIC) to insure bank deposits. The Social Security Act was a New Deal program to provide benefits to the elderly, children, and the disabled.

Other programs were short-lived but helped put Americans to work. These included the Civilian Conservation Corps, which built roads, trails, cabins, and campgrounds; the Public Works Administration, which built many new bridges, roads, and tunnels; and the Works Progress Administration (WPA), which built highways, cleaned up slums, and improved rural areas. The WPA hired writers, musicians, actors, and artists to conduct oral histories, write guidebooks, decorate public buildings with paintings and sculpture, organize orchestras and choruses for music, and perform in places where live theater had never been seen before.

MORE SLANG

hot: stolen

jam: trouble

the rumble: the news

that's the crop: that's all of it

gooseberry lay: stealing clothes from a clothesline

1920s TIDBIT

Photographers working for the WPA traveled all over the United States documenting living conditions.

See some of their photos at the Library of Congress.

MORE SLANG

left holding the bag: to be blamed

pipe down: stop talking

beat it: scram, get lost

During World War II, the United States fought against Germany's Adolf Hitler and his Nazi regime in Europe and Japan's Emperor Hirohito and his forces in the Pacific. Wars have an unending appetite for equipment and supplies, such as tanks, airplanes, clothing, food, and other necessities for fighting troops. As factories went into high production, suddenly there were more jobs than there were people to do them. Combined with the New Deal programs, this finally brought the United States out of the Great Depression. By the 1950s, the country enjoyed a postwar boom that felt like a more controlled version of the Roaring Twenties.

MAKING MODERN AMERICA

The Roaring Twenties were a time of great optimism, excitement, and the feeling that life was wonderful and would only get better. It was also the birth, in many ways, of America as it is today. Many of the things that modern Americans can't imagine living without—consumer credit (credit cards and installment loans), a culture firmly based on consumer buying and selling, and households with the latest modern and technological conveniences—are here today because they had their start in the 1920s.

The importance of cars in American life began in the 1920s and has only increased since then. Cars gave Americans a way to live in suburban neighborhoods and commute to the cities for work. Cars also gave them access to areas beyond their homes for entertainment and shopping.

Cars long ago displaced trains as a common method of transportation. Because buses and trolleys are largely limited to urban areas, many Americans are dependent on cars to get to well-paying jobs or affordable stores.

Many other modern institutions got their start in the 1920s, mostly in terms of mass culture and entertainment. These include the record charts that track the popularity of songs, book clubs that offer popular titles at reduced prices, a new emphasis on spectator sports such as football and baseball, and the widespread importance of radio and movie entertainment.

These entertainment institutions also helped to forge a common popular culture for Americans that continues today. People were once mostly confined to their own small region of the country. They had little knowledge of what people in the other parts of the country might be buying, reading, or enjoying. That all changed during the 1920s, when radio and movies helped to spread news, advertising, trends, and even attitudes.

CATCH A FILM?

Movie attendance went from just 50 million a week in 1920 to 90 million a week in 1929, when three-fourths of the U.S. population went to the movies every week. These are the 15 most popular movies of the 1920s:

Battleship Potemkin, 1925
Sunrise, 1927
Wings, 1927
The Phantom of the Opera, 1925
The Jazz Singer, 1927
Safety Last! 1923
London After Midnight, 1927
Dr. Jekyll and Mr. Hyde, 1920
The Man Who Laughs, 1928
Nosferatu, 1922
Metropolis, 1927
The Kid, 1921
The Cabinet of Dr. Caligari, 1920
The Gold Rush, 1925
The General, 1926

Radio also spread racial and cultural caricatures. Stereotypes about African Americans were found in radio shows such as *Amos 'n Andy*. Ethnic stereotypes included Italian gangsters and tightfisted Jewish characters.

Radio and film, as well as the introduction of the record player, helped to spread the craze for jazz and blues music. In sports, Americans began to follow "heroes" such as boxer Jack Dempsey, as well as root for national baseball and football teams.

ECONOMIC UPS AND DOWNS

Some of the negative legacies of the 1920s are also still with Americans today. Consumer credit overwhelms many families, which end up with the burden of credit card debt, car payments, and mortgages that keep them on the verge of financial collapse. In the early 2000s, many Americans purchased expensive homes with high-rate adjustable mortgages, which banks had freely given to many people who could not afford them. Many of these mortgages were new, nontraditional loans for buyers who could not qualify for traditional home loans.

Buyers no longer had to produce as many guarantees that their incomes could support a mortgage payment. Interest rates were low, making homes seem more affordable for first-time buyers. Because the real estate market was growing, home prices were rising. Even though real estate values were high, many home buyers assumed values would continue to rise and they'd be able to sell their houses at a profit. However, in 2001 and then again in 2008, the United States suffered economic downturns.

Many of the elements of mass culture and entertainment that were created in the 1920s are a permanent part of American life today.

TRENDS TODAY

The Internet and MP3 technology popularize musical trends and tastes just as radio once did. Movies are still one of the more popular forms of entertainment, even if people tend to download or stream them at home on their televisions or computers rather than go to the movie theaters.

The 2001 downturn was largely due to enthusiastic investing in technology. Many people bought stock in Internet and technology companies whose value seemed destined to rise higher and higher with no end in sight. When that end inevitably came these companies lost value, which led to sell-offs and bankruptcies for many of them.

The 2008 downturn was caused by a bubble in the housing market. Interest rates increased so much that many homeowners could no longer afford their rising monthly payments. This led to foreclosures and overall falling housing values. In many cases, people ended up owing more on their mortgages than their homes were worth.

Banks became afraid to loan money to each other because they were losing money on foreclosures. The government was forced to bail out some of the failing banks and mortgage companies. Remember what happened after the 1920s when so many banks closed? No one wanted the Great Depression to happen again. The economic downturn led to higher unemployment, which, despite government efforts to correct the economy's problems, was still high in 2012.

Just as the enthusiastic, optimistic years of the 1920s led to the grim, difficult years of the Great Depression, the United States will always cycle through good times and not-so-good times, from bubble to bust. A bubble is a state of booming activity in one part of the economy that often ends suddenly, like a bubble bursting.

WILL TIMES "ROAR" AGAIN?

In the years since the Roaring Twenties, the United States has been through many economic ups and downs. But Americans continue to have an unquenchable optimism for the future, even as an awareness of the past guides their everyday lives. And that's the greatest legacy of American history.

The 1920s were more prosperous in the United States than in any other nation of the world. Because it had access to many natural resources, such as coal and iron, it did not need to buy raw materials from other countries for its manufacturing. This made the U.S. economy stronger.

Many European countries had to take out loans from the United States during WWI. After the war, repayments and interest sent to America created an unbalanced cash flow. Many European countries were also struggling to rebuild their economies after WWI. Even when they regained their manufacturing production levels, they could not compete with the United States or find enough new markets for goods.

AFTER WWI, THE COUNTRIES STRUCK A DEAL.

WHILE TIMES "ROARED" IN THE U.S. IN THE 1920s...

The 1929 stock market crash affected the entire world, not just the United States, since so much trade had depended on the United States. Many U.S. investors were forced to pull out of European investments. Congress raised tariffs on foreign goods, which made them more expensive and less attractive to U.S. consumers. Tariffs decreased the U.S. market for foreign goods. In reaction, European markets increased their own tariffs even more, making it harder for U.S. companies to sell goods overseas.

As European banks also collapsed, Germany was no longer able to repay its debts from WWI. Countries that relied on German payments to fund their own governments—including the United States—struggled as a result. Unemployment rose across Europe.

Economic struggles also led to political struggles. In Austria and Germany, which were hardest hit by the spreading depression, Adolf Hitler's Nazi Party was able to gain strength through its policies for expansion and a better economy for Germans. This set Europe on the path to World War II.

1920s TIDBIT

After WWI, the United States surpassed Great Britain as the world's economic leader. While America's natural resources were a source of strength, Europe's lack of natural resources was a source of weakness. Many nations maintained high tariffs in the 1920s to protect their own manufacturers. This raised prices, cut world trade, and further weakened the world economy.

A tariff is a tax on goods coming into or leaving a country. Governments use tariffs to protect their own manufacturers from competition from foreign goods.

THEY SAY HE WAS A HERO...

...AND NOW HE BEGS JUST LIKE US.

ACROSS THE OCEAN THEY CONTINUED TO SUFFER.

HE SAID HE HAD "THE SOLUTION."

TO PLOW OR NOT TO PLOW?

The Dust Bowl of the 1930s took place because of the farming methods used by farmers in the 1920s. New technology and easy credit brought tractors to the farm. Farmers plowed up more and more land to plant crops. When drought came, the soil easily dried up and blew away, causing the black blizzards of dust. This experiment will test the difference between plowed and unplowed soil. How well does each retain surface moisture? It is the surface moisture that helps keep soil from blowing away. The moisture testing needs to be done on a day when it is not raining or snowing. The warmer and sunnier the day, the faster and clearer your results will be.

NOTE: Because this project uses a lot of dirt and water, you will need a good outdoor test area, one that can easily be washed after you are done testing. You should also wear clothing that you don't mind getting dirty!

- **First, prepare your field model in the plastic tray.** What would a field of soil that had been undisturbed for many years be like? This is what you want to try to recreate. Fill the plastic tray evenly with soil until it is about one-half to two-thirds full. Undisturbed soil is not light and fluffy—it has been compacted over time. How can you make your soil compact? Slowly pour about 2 cups (473 milliliters) of water evenly over the compacted soil. Press down firmly on the soil and wait a minute or two.

- **Press the probe of the soil moisture meter all the way down to the bottom of the soil in one corner of the tray.** If the moisture reading is less than 8 on a scale of 1 to 10, remove the probe and add approximately ¼ cup (59 milliliters) of water, to that corner. Press down firmly on the soil and wait a minute or two.

- **Repeat until all areas of the tray are around an 8 on the moisture meter.** Press down firmly on all the soil one last time. What does adding water and compacting the soil several times imitate in nature?

- **On one half of your field, how can you imitate plowing up the soil?** Be sure to plow all the way to the bottom of the tray as you turn the soil over. This half of the tray will be your model of a plowed field.

- **Leave the soil on the other half of your field undisturbed.** What would a real field that had been undisturbed be—bare soil or covered by plant material? To imitate this, cover this half with a thin layer of mulch or dead plant matter. This half of the tray will be your model of a no-till field.

PROJECT CONTINUES ON NEXT PAGE ▶

Ideas for Supplies ▼

- plastic box or tray
- soil
- soil moisture meter, available at some hardware and garden stores and from online sellers
- hand trowel
- mulch, such as straw, dead plant matter, or grass clippings
- measuring cups
- sturdy box or stool
- permanent marker
- clock
- lab notebook

• **What happens to the two halves of the field when the sun has time to heat the soil?** Place your tray in a warm, sunny area and take your first measurements right away. Use the moisture meter to measure the moisture in the top, middle, and bottom of the plowed field model. Why do you want to measure at different levels in the soil? Create a data table to record these measurements over time, beginning with the first measurement for time equal to "0."

TIME	TOP	MIDDLE	BOTTOM	AVERAGE
0				
1 hour				
2 hours				
3 hours				
4 hours				
5 hours				

• **At the same time, take these measurements on the side of your field that has not been "plowed."** Record your measurements on another data table. Repeat these same measurements on each side every hour for the next five hours.

• **Analyze your readings.** For each hour in each data table, calculate the average moisture meter reading. How would you graph these moisture readings for each field model? Looking at your data, which field model retained moisture the best?

> To investigate more, consider what different levels of soil moisture might mean on a farm. What would happen to your soil if you aimed a fan at it? What if you turned the fan on high? How does this help explain what happened during the Dust Bowl?

YESTERDAY AND TODAY

Inquire & Investigate

It is interesting to compare the cost of living in the 1920s to the cost of living today. One way to do that is by comparing average incomes and the cost of everyday goods. Do you spend the same amount of money on things today that people did in the 1920s?

- **Research 10 average household goods or food products that were around in the 1920s and are still around today.** Using 1920s advertising and other price sources, can you find out what these products cost in the 1920s?

- **Using the Consumer Price Index inflation calculator at data.bls.gov/cgi-bin/cpicalc.pl, calculate what these 1920s prices would equal in today's dollars.** Can you find the current prices for these same goods today? Figure out how to chart your findings, comparing the three sets of data.

- **Now find the data for wages paid for five common occupations in the 1920s.** Ideas include teachers, coal miners, policemen, bus drivers, or secretaries. Can you find the wages for these same jobs today? Make a chart of your findings, comparing the wages from the two time periods.

- **Looking at your charts, what conclusions can you draw about the cost of living as related to income in the 1920s and now?** Who had the better economic position, the people living in the 1920s or people living now?

> To investigate more, make the same comparison between today and another era in U.S. history, such as the 1930s Great Depression era or during WWII.

PRICES AND WAGES GUIDES

How much did things cost in the 1920s? How much did people earn?

You can find lots of information on wages in the 1920s here.

HOT OFF THE PRESS

There was plenty of panic when the stock market crashed in October 1929, but many people tried to calm the public by assuring them that the market would soon correct itself. As a result, there were two different approaches in the newspaper journalism of the time.

1920s TIDBIT

Some journalists reported on what had happened to the stock market and the huge negative impact it would have on the economy. Others tried to bolster the public's attitude and convey the feeling that things were fine.

- **Find two newspaper articles dating from the days immediately after the 1929 stock market crash.** One should reflect the general public's feeling of panic and shock based on the crash and its implications. The other should reflect a view that things would correct themselves and be fine.

- **What difference do you see in tone and approach?** What do you think each author is trying to convey to the public? Knowing that the country was actually about to enter a long and devastating depression, how do you feel about the optimistic article? Do you think it might have been possible to alleviate some of the Depression's impact if there had been a more widespread attempt to fix the economy after the crash?

- **Write a factual reporting article about the crash and what happened as a result.** Then write an article minimizing the panic. Stress that it's possible to move ahead and repair some of the damage.

To investigate more, find two articles about the beginning of the economic downturn of the 2000s, one that is optimistic and another that is pessimistic. From the vantage point of 2014, which article seems to be more accurate?

abstract: existing more in thought and ideas than in reality.

adjustable mortgage: a home loan with an interest rate that can increase, costing the homeowner more money.

advent: the arrival of a person, event, or thing.

advertising: to bring the public's attention to a product or person or idea by pointing out something good about it. Advertising is often used to sell products.

advocate: to publicly support something.

affiliation: a connection to something.

alcoholism: an addiction to drinking alcoholic beverages.

amendment: a correction, addition, or change to the U.S. constitution.

American Civil Liberties Union (ACLU): an organization founded in 1920 to defend the civil rights of all Americans.

American dream: an American ideal that says material prosperity means success.

anarchist: a person who does not believe that government and laws are necessary, and wants to abolish them.

antibiotic: a medicine made from bacteria meant to treat infection.

antitrust laws: laws that promote business competition and prevent monopolies.

antiwar: against war.

arbitration: the process where someone settles a dispute between other people.

arms race: a competition between countries over the quality and quantity of their weapons.

artillery: large-caliber guns that are used in war.

assembly line: an arrangement of workers and tasks in a factory to make assembling products faster.

atheist: a person who doesn't believe in any supreme being, such as God.

aviation: the business or practice of flying airplanes and helicopters.

bankruptcy: the status of a person or business that can't pay its debts.

bohemian: a person with casual or unconventional social habits.

Bolshevik Revolution: a revolution in Russia in 1917 during which the Bolsheviks overthrew the Russian Social Democratic Workers' Party, which had just recently overthrown the royal government.

Bolshevik: a member of the left-wing majority group of the Russian Social Democratic Workers' Party, later known as a communist.

bond: an interest-earning loan from an individual to a company that needs the money to operate.

bootlegger: someone who makes, distributes, or sells liquor illegally.

bribe: to pay someone to make a decision or act dishonestly.

business: the act of making, buying, or selling goods or services in exchange for money.

campaign: a connected series of activities designed to bring about a result, such as electing a person to public office or selling a product to a large number of people.

capitalism: an economy in which people, not the government, own the factories, ships, and land used in the production and distribution of goods.

caricature: an exaggeration of certain characteristics.

census: an official count of people living in an area.

character: the qualities of a person, or a person in a play, novel or debate.

Glossary

citizen: a person who legally belongs to a country and has the rights and protection of that country.

civil rights: the rights that every person should have regardless of his or her sex, race, or religion.

Civil Rights era: a nationwide movement for racial equality in the 1950s and 1960s.

Civil War: the war in the United States, from 1861 to 1865, between the states in the North and the slave-owning states in the South.

civilian: a person who is not a soldier.

commercial: sold to the consumer for a profit.

communism: an economy in which the government owns everything used in the production and distribution of goods.

competition: trying to get or win something that someone else is trying to get or win.

condense: to remove water from a substance to make it more concentrated.

Congress: a group of people who represent the states and make laws for the country.

conservative: traditional, favoring keeping things the same, cautious about accepting changes or new ideas.

constitution: a document containing the basic laws and beliefs of a country.

constitutionality: aligned with the principles set forth in the U.S. Constitution.

consumer credit: a line of credit for personal use, usually extended through credit cards.

consumer: a person who buys goods and services.

consumer goods: items, such as food and clothing, that people can buy to serve their own needs.

contraception: strategies for preventing pregnancy.

controversial: causing the public to argue over the issue.

corruption: the dishonest or illegal behavior of people in power.

corset: a tightly fitting woman's undergarment.

cost of living: the amount of money needed to support an average person at a certain time.

credit: paying for something later or over time.

crop: a plant grown by farmers for harvest.

cultural identity: the behavior, interests, desires, and passions of a group of people.

culture: a group of people and their beliefs and way of life.

dadaism: an art movement that went against traditional ideas of beauty and cultural value.

debt: when a person or business owes money.

dialogue: conversation.

disabled: having a physical or mental condition that limits movement, sensation, or activities.

disarmament: to reduce or withdraw military forces and weapons.

discrimination: the unfair treatment of a person or a group of people because of their identity.

disillusionment: disappointment from finding out that something isn't as good as it was thought to be.

disposable income: the amount of money a person has after paying taxes and expenses.

distill: to heat a mash of grains until it becomes a gas, then cool it to condense the gas into a liquid—alcohol.

distribution of wealth: the way the income of a country is divided among its people.

domestic issue: a problem that only affects the United States.

drought: a period of time without enough rainfall.

Dust Bowl: the region of the south central United States that was damaged in the 1920s and '30s by persistent dust storms that killed off crops and livestock.

economic downturn: when a country's business activity starts to shrink.

economy: the wealth and resources of a country.

efficient: wasting as little time as possible completing a task.

eliminate: to get rid of.

emotion: a strong feeling.

empower: to give someone authority and power.

entice: to make attractive or tempting.

entrepreneur: a person who creates or operates a business, usually at financial risk.

epitome: someone or something that is a perfect example of a certain type or quality.

era: a period of history marked by distinctive people or events.

ethical: acting in a way that upholds someone's belief in right and wrong.

ethnic: sharing customs, languages, and beliefs.

evict: to remove someone from a property.

evolution: the belief that man evolved from lower orders of animals.

exuberant: filled with energy and excitement.

factory: a place where goods are made.

feminist: a person who believes men and women should have equal rights and opportunities.

ferment: to go through a chemical change that results in the creation of alcohol.

fertile: land that is rich in nutrients and good for growing crops.

financial: relating to money.

financing: paying for expensive items over a set period of time instead of all at once.

flapper: a fashionable young woman of the 1920s who did not conform to old standards of behavior.

force: to make someone do something.

foreclose: when a bank takes back a mortgaged property because payments have not been made.

foreign policy: the way the government deals with other nations.

free trade: unrestricted trade between countries.

frugality: taking care not to waste money or resources.

fundamentalist: someone whose religion believes in the literal interpretation of the Bible.

gangster: a member of a gang of violent criminals.

garter: an elastic band worn around the leg to hold up a stocking.

goods: things to use or sell.

Great Depression: the economic turndown that began with the stock market crash in 1929 and continued through the 1930s.

heritage: a culture passed down through generations.

human rights: the rights that belong to all people, such as freedom from torture, the right to live, and freedom from slavery.

icon: a person or thing that grows to represent a larger idea.

immigrant: a person who settles in a new country.

immigration: moving to a new country to live there.

improvisation: to perform with little or no preparation.

industrial: the large-scale production of goods, especially in factories.

Industrial Revolution: the period of time when civilization moved from agriculture to industry, and many new inventions and machines were used.

innovation: a new device, idea, or method.

Glossary

installment plan: a credit system where payment is made in small amounts over time.

intellectual: involving serious thought.

interest: money paid regularly at a particular rate for the use of credit.

international: involving two or more countries.

intolerance: the unwillingness to share rights with certain groups of people.

invention: a new tool or machine or way of doing something.

invest: to commit money in the hope of a larger future return.

isolate: to be separate from others.

isolationism: the policy of remaining apart from other countries and not getting involved in their affairs.

Jazz Age: a period of time marked by prosperity, innovation, and changing social norms, when jazz music and dance was popular.

jazz: popular music that originated among African Americans in New Orleans in the late nineteenth century. It is characterized by syncopated rhythms and improvisation.

Ku Klux Klan: a club organized in the South after the Civil War. It used violence against African Americans and other minority groups.

labor movement: an organized effort from workers to improve their wages and working conditions.

landlord: a person who rents land or housing to a tenant.

League of Nations: an organization created in 1919 intended to prevent future wars.

legacy: something handed down from the past that has a long-lasting impact.

leisure: free time.

liberal: believing government should actively support social and political change. Open to change and new ideas.

lifestyle: the way a person or group lives.

literature: written works— poems, plays, and novels.

local: located or living nearby.

Lost Generation: the generation that came of age during or after WWI, many of whom were disillusioned by the war.

mainstream: the popular thoughts and opinions of the majority of a group.

manufacture: to make something by machine in a factory.

manufacturer: a company that makes a product.

manufacturing: to make large quantities of products in a factory.

margin call: a demand from a broker that an investor who bought on margin deposit more money to cover possible losses.

market: the opportunity to buy or sell goods or services.

mass production: the production of a large quantity of goods, often made on an assembly line.

materialistic: concerned with owning things.

media: the radio stations, television stations, and newspapers through which information is communicated to the public.

menial: boring work that does not require skill and pays very little money.

merchandising: arranging products in a store to make them sell better.

merchant: someone who buys and sells goods for a profit.

middle class: the group of people made of professionals and skilled workers and their families.

migrant: someone who moves from place to place, usually to find work.

migrate: to move from one area to another.

minority: a group of people, such as African Americans, that is smaller than or different from the larger group.

modern: relating to the present time, a style that is new or different, or based on the newest information or technology; the opposite of traditional.

modernist: a person who supports the ideals of modernism, which in the 1920s included women's rights, civil liberties, and technological advancements.

modest: not showing much of a person's body.

monopoly: having exclusive control over a commodity or service in business.

morality: the social rules of conduct.

morals: a person's standards of behavior or belief.

mortgage: a loan taken out for housing or land.

national: related to the entire country.

national debt: the total amount of money a country owes.

negotiation: a formal discussion between two sides that want to reach an agreement.

newsreel: a short film of news or current events, shown before a regular movie in a theater.

optimism: hopefulness and confidence about the future.

oral history: history that is passed down through generations by stories told out loud.

organized crime: illegal behavior carried out by groups of people in a systematic way to earn money.

pacifist: someone who does not believe in violence or war.

patriotism: the love that citizens feel for their country.

percentage: a portion of the whole.

perishable: likely to decay or go bad quickly, especially food.

petticoat: a women's loose undergarment worn under a dress or skirt.

policy: an action or rule adopted by a country.

political: relating to a country's government.

politician: someone who works in the government as an elected official.

popular culture: the mainstream ideas, images, music, literature, movies, and other phenomenon of a particular society during a particular time.

population: the people of an area or country.

postwar: after the war.

poverty: the state of being very poor.

poverty line: the minimum level of income necessary to buy the basic needs for living.

prejudice: a negative opinion of someone that isn't based on knowledge or experience.

product: something that is made or grown to be sold or used.

production: the large-scale making of something.

productive: hard working.

profit: the money made by selling an item or service for more than it cost.

Prohibition: the period of time from 1920 to 1933 when the sale of alcoholic beverages was banned—or prohibited—in the United States.

proliferation: an increase in the number or amount of something.

promote: to make people aware of something, such as a new product, through advertising; to make something more popular or well known.

prosperity: a state of success, wealth, or comfort.

psychoanalyst: a person who helps people with mental and emotional problems by having the patient talk about dreams, feelings, and memories.

public relations: the practice of creating a good public image for a person or company.

race: a group of people that shares distinct physical qualities, such as skin color.

racism: negative opinions or treatment of people based on race.

radical: a person with extreme political or social views.

ratify: to give official approval of something, such as a constitutional amendment.

realism: an artistic style in which images represent the scene as it actually looks.

recession: a temporary economic slowdown.

reconnaissance: the military observation or investigation of an enemy.

Reconstruction: the period of time after the Civil War when the United States was reorganized and reunited.

Red Scare: a period of time when many people were afraid of communists.

reformer: a person devoted to bringing about social change.

regime: a government or system, especially one that has firm control over people.

regulate: to control by rules or laws.

resource: something a country has that supports its wealth, such as food, money, and land.

revivalism: a form of religious activity that revives or refreshes religious feeling.

risky: involving the possibility of something bad or unpleasant happening.

ritual: an action performed in a certain way.

rocketry: the study of rocket design and use.

role: the expected behavior and characteristics of an individual.

rural: relating to people who live in the country or on farms.

segregation: the policy of keeping people of different races separate from each other.

Semitic: Jewish

sequence: the particular order in which movements or events follow each other.

sharecropper: a tenant farmer who gives a landlord part of each crop as rent.

shortage: not enough of something for everyone.

social freedom: the ability of an individual to behave as he or she wishes within the law. For a woman in the 1920s, this might mean working, driving, choosing a dance partner, or traveling alone.

society: a group of people with shared laws, traditions, and values.

speakeasy: an illegal and secret liquor store or nightclub.

speculation: making investments in the hope of making a large profit, but with the risk of a large loss.

standard of living: the amount of wealth and material goods available to a person.

statistics: numbers that show facts about a subject.

stenographer: someone who writes down what people are saying, usually in a courtroom.

stereotype: to make a judgment about a group of individuals.

still: a device used to process wheat into alcohol.

stock: ownership shares in a company.

stock market: a market where stock is bought and sold.

stockbroker: a person who buys and sells stock on behalf of clients.

strike: when everyone walks off the job to protest working conditions or pay.

subconscious: the part of the mind below the level of conscious perception.

suburban: having to do with living areas at the edges of towns and cities.

superficial: shallow, not caring very much about anything serious.

surplus: more than what is needed.

surrealism: an art movement that tried to release the power of the unconscious mind using strange and dreamlike images.

symbol: an image that stands for something else.

synchronized: occurring or operating at the same time or rate.

syncopation: a shift in music where a weak beat is accented, creating an unusual rhythm.

talkie: a movie with a soundtrack.

tariff: a tax or duty paid on imported or exported goods.

tax evasion: not paying taxes owed to the government.

technology: tools, methods, and systems used to solve a problem or do work.

temperance: the practice of drinking little or no alcohol.

tenant: a person who rents land or housing from a landlord.

thrift: using money carefully.

traditional: a belief, custom, or way of doing things that has been passed from generation to generation for a long time.

traditionalist: a person who believes in traditional ideals, including hard work, agriculture, and church.

transition: a period of change.

treaty: a formal agreement between countries.

trend: what is popular at a certain point in time.

unconstitutional: not in accordance with the ideals of the U.S. constitution.

unemployment: the state of joblessness.

unemployment rate: the number of people who don't have jobs in a certain area or time.

uniform: always the same in character or degree.

union: an organization of workers formed to protect their rights.

urban: relating to cities or towns.

values: a strongly held belief about what is valuable, important, or acceptable.

veto: an official vote of "no" from the person in power.

virtuous: having high moral standards.

wages: payment for work.

warrant: an official document authorizing someone's arrest.

workflow: the sequence of a piece of work moving from start to finish.

workforce: the people in an area or country who want to work.

BOOKS

Temperance and Prohibition: The Movement to Pass Anti-Liquor Laws in America. Mark Beyer, Rosen Publishing, 2006.

Popular Culture: 1920–1939. Jane Bingham, Heinemann-Raintree, 2012.

Prosecuting Trusts: The Courts Break Up Monopolies in America. Bernadette Brexel, Rosen Publishing, 2006.

The 1920s Decade in Photos: The Roaring Twenties. Jim Corrigan, Enslow Publishers, 2010.

Duke Ellington: His Life in Jazz with 21 Activities. Stephanie Stein Crease, Chicago Review Press, 2009.

Prohibition. John M. Dunn, Lucent Books, 2010.

Louis Armstrong and the Jazz Age. Dan Elish, Children's Press, 2008.

A Look at the Eighteenth and Twenty-First Amendments: The Prohibition and Sale of Intoxicating Liquors. Amy Graham, Enslow Publishers, 2007.

Roaring Twenties: Almanac and Primary Sources. Kelly King Howes, UXL, 2005.

Roaring 20's Reference Library: Biographies. Kelly King Howes, UXL, 2005.

Double Cheeseburgers, Quiche, and Vegetarian Burritos: American Cooking from the 1920s Through Today. Loretta Frances Ichord, Millbrook Press, 2006.

The History of Jazz. Stuart A. Kallen, Lucent Books, 2012.

The Prohibition Era in American History. Suzanne Lieurance, Enslow Publishers, 2003.

World War I and the Roaring Twenties: 1914–1928. Tim McNeese, Chelsea House, 2010.

Fabulous Fashions of the 1920s. Felicia Lowenstein Niven, Enslow Publishers, 2011.

America in the 1920s. Michael J. O'Neal, Facts on File, 2005.

America Has Fun: The Roaring Twenties. Sean Stewart Price, Raintree, 2008.

Exploring Cultural History: Living in 1920s America. Myra et al., Weatherly, Greenhaven Press, 2005.

Teetotalers and Saloon Smashers: The Temperance Movement and Prohibition. Richard Worth, Enslow Publishers, 2009.

PLACES TO VISIT

President Calvin Coolidge Historic Site
historicsites.vermont.gov/directory/coolidge

The Henry Ford Museum
thehenryford.org/museum/index.aspx

The Crime Museum
crimemuseum.org

National Capital Radio & Television Museum
ncrtv.org

American Jazz Museum
americanjazzmuseum.org

WEBSITES

Best of History Websites: The Roaring Twenties
besthistorysites.net/index.php/american-history/1900/roaring-20s

Digital History: The Formation of Modern American Mass Culture
digitalhistory.uh.edu/disp_textbook.cfm?smtID=2&psid=3397

The People History: Events From the 1920s
thepeoplehistory.com/1920s.html

The National Archives: The Volstead Act
archives.gov/education/lessons/volstead-act

The Lawless Decade: A Pictorial History of the 1920s
lawlessdecade.net

The Library of Congress: Prosperity and Thrift: The Coolidge Era
lcweb2.loc.gov/ammem/coolhtml/coolhome.html

A Biography of America: The Twenties
learner.org/biographyofamerica/prog20/feature/index.html

Edsitement: Postwar Disillusionment and the Quest for Peace, 1921-1929
edsitement.neh.gov/lesson-plan/postwar-disillusionment-and-quest-peace-1921-1929#sect-background

Jazz: A Film by Ken Burns
pbs.org/jazz/index.htm

Clash of Cultures in the 1910s and 1920s
ehistory.osu.edu/osu/mmh/clash/default.htm

Federal Deposit Insurance Corporation (FDIC): The Learning Bank
fdic.gov/about/learn/learning/index.html

American History USA: Working and Voting: Women in the 1920s
americanhistoryusa.com/working-voting-women-1920s

Index

R

radio, vii, 2, 9, 11, 18–19, 45–47, 79, 99–100
Ray, Man, 62
Red Scare, 29–32
religion, 12, 28, 48–49
Roaring Twenties
    culture in, vi–vii, 2, 4, 11–12, 45–47, 50, 58–73, 79, 97, 98–100 (see also art; clothing and fashion; lifestyles and values; literature; movies; music; radio)
    definition and description of, 2, 4
    economy in, vii, 6–20, 76–89, 92–98, 100–103, 107–108 (see also consumerism/consumer credit; debt; employment; money; poverty and hardship; standard of living; stock market; taxes/tariffs)
    end of, 92–108
    inventions and innovations in, vi, 4, 6, 7, 33, 40–55, 60, 70
    politics and government in, vi, vii, 8–9, 20, 22–38, 51, 64–65, 77, 82, 85, 93, 96, 101, 103
    Prohibition in, vi, 4, 22–28, 36–38, 77, 88
rockets, vii, 49–50, 54–55
Roosevelt, Franklin, 97
Russia, 24, 30–31

S

Sacco, Ferdinando Nicola, vi, vii, 31, 32, 34–35
St. Valentine's Day Massacre, vii, 28, 38
Savage, Augusta, 65
Scopes, John/Scopes trial, vii, 48–49

sharecropping, 80–83
skyscrapers, 43, 52–53
slang terms, 65, 67, 72, 73, 77, 93, 94, 97, 98
Smith, Bessie, 67
Social Security Act, 97
space exploration, vii, 49–50, 54–55
speakeasies, 26–27, 65
sports, vi, 99, 100
standard of living, 7, 14, 16, 82, 97, 107. See also money; poverty and hardship
Steinbeck, John, 98
stock market, vii, 6, 8, 13, 16–17, 77, 92–95, 97, 101, 103, 108
Strauss, Samuel, 10

T

taxes/tariffs, 8, 37, 77, 103
Terkel, Studs, 93

U

unions, 84, 85, 97
urban areas. See cities

V

values. See lifestyles and values
Van Der Zee, James, 65
Vanzetti, Bartolomeo, vi, vii, 31, 32, 34–35
Volstead Act, 25, 26

W

Walgreen Drugs/Walgreens Pharmacy, 12, 13
Waring, Laura Wheeler, 65

Whiteman, Paul, 67
women
    clothing and fashion of, 2, 4, 46, 58, 59, 84
    employment of, 2, 4, 60, 85
    as flappers, 4, 59–60, 61, 73
    role and lifestyles of, vi, 2, 4, 58–60, 61, 70
    temperance movement support by, 23–24
    voting rights of, vi, 4, 60
Women's Christian Temperance Union, 23
Wood, Beatrice, 62
Woolworth's, 12
work. See employment
Works Progress Administration, 97
World Trade Center, 52
World War I, vi, 3–4, 14, 30, 44, 60, 61, 77, 85, 102, 103
World War II, 97, 98, 103